THE AMERICAN SHAKERS AND THEIR FURNITURE

John G. Shea

THE AMERICAN SHAKERS AND THEIR FURNITURE

with measured drawings of museum classics

VAN NOSTRAND REINHOLD COMPANY

NEW YORK   CINCINNATI   TORONTO   LONDON   MELBOURNE

Printed in the United States of America

Published by Van Nostrand Reinhold Company
A division of Litton Educational Publishing, Inc.
135 West 50th Street, New York, NY 10020, U.S.A.

Van Nostrand Reinhold Limited
1410 Birchmount Road
Scarborough, Ontario M1P 2E7, Canada

Van Nostrand Reinhold Australia Pty. Ltd.
17 Queen Street
Mitcham, Victoria 3132, Australia

Van Nostrand Reinhold Company Limited
Molly Millars Lane
Wokingham, Berkshire, England

8   10   12   14   16   15   13   11   9   7

DEDICATION

This book is respectfully dedicated to the American Shakers, whose enduring and inspiring accomplishments have enriched the culture and industries of the United States ever since the start of this nation almost two hundred years ago. It is the timely privilege of this first edition to convey salutations to surviving Shakers of the two remaining communities, as they continue to conduct their communal affairs with the traditional Shaker virtues of piety, humility, industry, and kindness.

TO THE SHAKERS OF
CANTERBURY, NEW HAMPSHIRE:

Senior Sister Lillian Phelps
Ministry Eldress Marguerite Frost
Eldress Bertha Lindsay
Sister Alice M. Howland
Sister Ethel S. Hudson
Sister G. Miriam Wall

TO THE SHAKERS OF
SABBATHDAY LAKE, MAINE:

Eldress Gertrude M. Soule
Senior Sister Eleanor M. Philbrook
Sister R. Mildred Barker
Sister Marie F. Burgess
Sister Frances A. Carr
Sister Elizabeth L. Dunn
Sister Minnie E. Green
Sister Elsie A. McCool
Sister Ethel M. Peacock

PREFACE

It started at Pleasant Hill, Kentucky, where we went after witnessing the blast-off of Apollo 11 in Florida. Driving up from the South, we wondered what it would be like — a Shaker village fully restored with overnight accommodations for visitors in the very rooms the Shakers had occupied. We did not know what these accommodations would be like, but since Pleasant Hill is advertised as an *authentic* restoration, we expected to "rough it" in the austere nineteenth-century environment of the original Shakers.

We promptly discovered it wasn't going to be that way at all. We were given a spacious corner room in the Trustees' Building — the handsome brick guest dwelling that the Shakers built in 1839. Our first observation was that the room was abundantly air-conditioned. Then our eyes wandered from glossy simulations of Shaker furniture to a flickering focal point — a television set, styled strictly un-Shaker. The modern appointments, bright decor, and luxurious box-spring beds also seemed somewhat super-Shaker. And a handbill on the dresser informed us that during the evening we could attend a performance of Shakespeare selections. *Shakespeare's Shakers!* What next?

That evening we enjoyed a hearty Shaker dinner served by girls of the community, their mini-skirts shrouded in flowing Shaker garments. After dinner we went outdoors and strolled in the soft twilight. Here it was different. Along the gravel paths, with their bordering white picket fences, the magnificent old Shaker buildings still stand impregnable — unspoiled by tourist trappings.

As nightfall descended with crickets and cicadas chorusing in the dusk, we could hear the lowing of cattle in distant pastures. The tranquillity of this rural setting carried us back to the era of Shaker occupancy, which began in 1814. For here, in contrast to the noise and confusion of our electronic world, peace was restored to a pleasant place where the Shakers once lived, worked, and worshiped.

Our visit to Pleasant Hill marked the start of research that took us to the sites of twelve of the original Shaker communities, located in seven different states. We also visited most of the museums and other repositories of Shaker furniture and artifacts in cities and towns away from the original Shaker communities. All in all, we traveled some ten thousand miles visiting and revisiting Shaker places.

Since the Shakers had a habit of locating their communities in the most picturesque parts of the country, our travels provided exciting rewards. There were the lovely rolling hills in the bluegrass regions of Kentucky and the beautiful Berkshires of New York and Massachusetts, painted in vivid hues of autumn.

We recall one bright October afternoon driving along the Berkshire trail from Harvard to Hancock, Massachusetts. Each turn in the road produced fresh panoramas of foliage ablaze in myriads of brilliant colors. Fleecy clouds floated in azure skies. Streams and lakes rippled along the way, reflecting the deepest shades of blue. Here was nature at its breathtaking best — the perfection of God's work as witnessed and worshiped by the Believers whose communities were located in these regions.

Later, on a cold winter afternoon, we again visited the impeccably restored Hancock Shaker Village. Snow lay deep around the old buildings. But indoors, in the snug and cheerful "Great Cook Room" of the Brick Dwelling built in 1830, the atmosphere was blissfully serene. The afternoon sun streamed through the multipaned windows as we relaxed in Shaker rockers surrounded by furniture and appointments that the Shakers used, in this very room, during the past one hundred and forty years. The nostalgic furnishings and deep propriety of this charming room induced feelings of perfect contentment. Such feelings must have been experienced by the original Shaker occupants — and this may partially explain why they wanted to live together in rural communes isolated from the outside world.

Then, there were the people and bits of history we encountered along the way. We visited Bronson Alcott's "Con-Sociate" utopia, located on a scenic hillside at Fruitlands, near Harvard, Massachusetts. Here, perfectly restored, is the farmhouse where his daughter, Louisa May Alcott, author of *Little Men* and *Little Women,* may have done some of her early writing. Here too is the Shaker House, which the founder of Fruitlands Museums, Mrs. Clara Endicott Sears, had moved intact all the way from its original site at Shirley, Massachusetts. It is now authentically furnished with antiques and artifacts gathered from the original Shaker communities at Harvard and Shirley.

Fruitlands, with its comprehensive library and early American museums, is now maintained under direction of Mr. William Henry Harrison. Mr. and Mrs. Harrison were our cordial hosts at several luncheon meetings in their charming eighteenth-century home.

At luncheon one day, we talked about previous visits to the Golden Lamb Inn — Ohio's oldest hostelry. The Golden Lamb had provided lodgings for ten United States Presidents, including Mr. Harrison's great-great-grandfather. By coincidence, we had occupied the William Henry Harrison Room during our most recent visit — the historical distinction of the room was clearly inscribed on the door. As a result, we were visited by a plague of door-knockers, all eager to examine the room in which President Harrison slept.

The present Mr. Harrison was amused by our plight. We speculated on the possibilities of what might happen if *he,* garbed in his ancestor's gaitered garments and stovepipe hat, were to occupy the same room. We could picture the startled reactions of visitors if he slowly opened the creaking door and confronted them, in antique attire, with solemn greetings: "Yes, I am Mr. Harrison. Won't you please come in?"

As the research continued we traveled north to visit the two surviving Shaker communities at Sabbathday Lake, Maine, and Canterbury, New Hampshire. Here we were privileged to meet living Shakers. (As this book goes to press, there are only fifteen female Shakers still surviving. The last male Shaker, Brother Delmer C. Wilson, of the Sabbathday community, died in 1961.) These gallant ladies conduct their lives in the pious patterns of the past. Their gentle manners and soft voices still distinguish them from the "world's people" — although few people alive today would find themselves more profoundly at peace with the world.

Meanwhile, along with the pleasures of people and places to which this research related, there was also work to be done. Shaker documents, early records and reference books, required careful study; authors and authorities were consulted on the many aspects of Shaker life; hundreds of photographs had to be taken; and endless hours were devoted to the task of securing accurate measurements of Shaker designs.

The intimate handling and measuring of hundreds of pieces of Shaker furniture gave us a feeling of rapport with the original Shaker craftsmen. It was like looking over their shoulders as they performed their century-old miracles of skill. Having designed and built furniture with hand tools and simple machines, in the straightforward manner of the Shakers, we could comprehend *why* they did *what* they did. And their cleverness never ceased to amaze us.

Most impressive was the discipline of their workmanship — the economy of structure that produced strength even when all parts were lightly and delicately made. When lifting a chair, bench, or table, we were invariably surprised to find it weighed only about half as much as expected.

Shaker craftsmen rejected superfluity of materials as well as adornment. And the beauty of their work came only as a by-product of its strict adherence to functional requirements. Indeed their philosophy of design was aptly summarized in the simple statement of one of their elders: *"That which has in itself the highest use possesses the greatest beauty."*

Some contend that the hands of God were at work in the creation of Shaker designs — and that it was only through God's intimate guidance that such perfection could be attained. Certainly, the Shakers' religious beliefs did play an important part in providing the fundamental rules of procedure. Pure principles of functionalism, laid down in manifestoes and edicts of the Central Ministry, disciplined all their work. They were instructed to avoid nonessential ornamentation and "worldly ostentation" — and in this way they achieved a beauty of design that they did not deliberately seek.

So, the Shakers' religious beliefs did prescribe the virtues of functionalism during an era when the implications of this quality were not too commonly understood. Over one hundred years later, functional designs, devoid of nonessential embellishment, became the basis of Bauhaus design philosophy. And, of course, today we witness the development of this idea in contemporary construction. But the Shakers got there first — and considering the superb craftsmanship they invested in their effort, it may well be contended that their performance was supernaturally inspired.

In this book, we endeavor to present a cross-section of the Shakers' accomplishment as represented, in particular, by their furniture craftsmanship. To gain some understanding of this accomplishment it is first necessary to know something about the Shakers themselves — how they lived, worked and worshiped — with emphasis on the many useful enterprises in which they engaged.

The construction chapters of this book are intended to add depth to our understanding of Shaker furniture. Usually, books of furniture designs show only the furniture itself without penetrating into significant details of its construction. This seems too superficial. The museum-measured drawings of Chapters 5, 6, and 7 are included to make it possible to analyze the anatomy of Shaker design. They were prepared to expose the organs and arteries of Shaker construction — something photographs alone cannot do.

This is not projected as a "how-to-do-it" book. Hopefully, it is a "how-they-did-it" book — how the Shakers did their superlative deeds of craftsmanship over a century ago. But the dimensioned drawings do have a how-to purpose, too. Without such drawings, present and future generations of craftsmen might find it difficult to reproduce Shaker designs accurately. The drawings are intended to encourage reproduction, to avoid a kind of sterility that might otherwise be imposed on Shaker furniture — and that could be just as depleting to Shaker designs as celibacy was to the Shakers themselves. And nobody wants this to happen to their wonderful work.

John G. Shea
Greenwich, Connecticut
1971

ACKNOWLEDGMENTS

My sincere thanks go to the distinguished authors, Shaker authorities, museum curators, and other knowledgeable people with whom I have enjoyed such pleasant and productive relations during the course of Shaker research.

Listed chronologically, in the order of our meeting, my thanks go first to the noted author-historian **Mrs. Hazel Spencer Phillips.** Along with her excellent books, Mrs. Phillips, who is curator of the Warren County Historical Society Museum at Lebanon, Ohio, has written extensively on the Shakers and has collected their furniture and artifacts from nearby Union Village to form part of her attractive museum displays.

Also at Lebanon, Ohio, I had the pleasure of chatting with **Mr. Robert H. Jones,** who for many years was the active proprietor of the Golden Lamb Inn — Ohio's oldest hotel. The Golden Lamb is furnished with many Shaker antiques from Mr. Jones' valuable collection. For access to these, my thanks also go to **Mr. Jackson B. Reynolds,** present director of the Golden Lamb, who was my congenial host and helper during subsequent sessions of furniture measuring and photography.

Later, during a second visit to Ohio and Kentucky, I met **Miss Julia Neal,** author-director of the Western Kentucky University Museum. Miss Neal, who has written authoritatively on the western Shakers, made documentary material available and described Shaker pieces of the museum collection. During a subsequent visit to the Auburn Shaker Museum, located near the original Shaker community of South Union, Kentucky, I had the privilege of talking with the museum director, **Mrs. Curry C. Hall.** Mrs. Hall has devoted years to the collection of her extensive museum displays of western Shakeriana. For making available some of his excellent photographs of Shaker furniture, taken at both Kentucky museums, my thanks go to **Professor E. Ray Pearson** of the Illinois Institute of Technology.

Returning to the east, the first of many visits was made to the Shaker Museum at Old Chatham, New York. There I met its scholarly author-director, **Mr. Robert F. W. Meader.** Mr. Meader's extensive knowledge of the Shakers was a significant help to me, and I am most grateful to him for making museum facilities available for photography and measurement of the comprehensive and beautifully organized displays of Shaker furniture and artifacts. Also at Old Chatham I had the pleasure of discussing aspects of Shaker life with the knowledgeable and congenial founder of the museum, **Mr. John S. Williams.** At the same place, I learned much about the Shakers while chatting with **Mr. Clarence Williams,** who knew them well.

Moving over to Hancock Shaker Village, just across the Massachusetts line from Old Chatham, I met the curator, **Dr. Eugene Merrick Dodd,** who contributed important information on the life and works of the Hancock Shakers. The friendship of Dr. Dodd is one of the happy rewards of this research — and I am most grateful to him for reading and commenting on the first chapter of this book.

At nearby Pittsfield, Massachusetts, I was invited to visit the charming home of **Mrs. Edward Deming Andrews.** Mrs. Andrews and her late husband, **Dr. Edward Deming Andrews,** deserve the everlasting thanks of all who are interested in the Shakers. For these dedicated authors devoted decades of their lives to Shaker research and wrote several definitive books on the Shakers. Their private collection of Shaker antiques, which Mrs. Andrews showed me in her home, is augmented by the treasures of Shaker furniture and artifacts that she and Dr. Andrews acquired during their years of research and later made available to museums in this country and abroad.

Over on the other side of Massachusetts, at Harvard, I became a frequent visitor at Fruitlands Museums, which is directed by **Mr. William Henry Harrison,** great-great-grandson of the ninth President of the United States. Mr. Harrison and his charming wife were most helpful and delightfully hospitable during my many visits to the restored Shirley Shaker House and other interesting exhibits at Fruitlands.

Moving north, into Maine, I visited the Shaker Village at Sabbathday Lake, where I had the privilege of meeting my first real Shaker — **Sister Mildred Barker.** Sister Mildred, a bright and energetic lady, guided me through the exhibits of original Shaker furniture and artifacts, telling me about the history of the community and waiting patiently while I performed my photographic chores. Also at Sabbathday Lake, I am grateful to the master craftsman **Mr. Gus Schwerdtfeger** for furnishing detailed measurements of typical pieces of Shaker furniture.

My second meeting with living Shakers occurred at Canterbury Shaker Village in New Hampshire. Here I met **Eldress Bertha Lindsay,** who introduced me to other Shaker sisters. Eldress Bertha and her colleagues — all charming and gentle ladies — graciously described the historical background of their one-hundred-and-seventy-eight-year-old community and guided my photography of the venerable Shaker buildings and furniture.

As well as the many pleasant contacts made at Shaker communities and adjoining museums, I am also grateful to the directors and curators of national, state, and city museums, who were most cooperative in making information and photographs available. These include **Dr. Grose Evans,** Curator of the Index of American Design at the National Art Galleries in Washington, D.C.; **Mr. Robert Bishop** and **Mrs. Katherine Hagler** of the Department of Decorative Arts at the Henry Ford Museum, Dearborn, Michigan; **Mr. John A. H. Sweeney** and **Miss Elizabeth S. Hamlin** of the Henry Francis du Pont Museum at Winterthur, Delaware; **Mr. John S. Watson,** History Curator of the New York State Educational Department (Museum), Albany, New York; **Mrs. Philippa Bishop** of the American Museum at Bath, England; **Mr. Sterling D. Emerson,** Curator of the Shelburne Museum at Shelburne, Vermont; and **Dr. Roman Drazniowsky,** Map Curator at the American Geographical Society in New York City.

To those who worked most closely with me in preparation of book manuscript, special thanks go to **Mr. Joseph A. Romeo,** the talented artist-draftsman who prepared precise pen-and-ink renderings of my measured drawings; **Mrs. Carol Wright Shea,** my artist daughter-in-law, who did the delightful pen-sketches of Shaker smallcraft, and my sister, **Miss May Frances Shea,** who, with usual efficiency, took care of secretarial details and final typing of manuscript.

J.G.S.

CONTENTS

CHAPTER I

SHAKER CREED, CUSTOMS, COLONIZATION, AND INDUSTRIES

Hands to Work and Hearts to God. Mother Ann Lee's admonition induced many craft activities, including hand weaving of beautiful Shaker fabrics. *Photo courtesy Index of American Design, Washington, D.C.*

Shaker Creed, Customs, Colonization, and Industries

She came from England in 1774, with eight faithful followers all of whom were convinced she was Christ Incarnate. With her disciples she had embarked on the frail ship *Mariah* at Liverpool, on May 10, 1774. The three months' voyage across the boiling Atlantic was no less stormy than the persecutions that had been provoked by their frantic religious rituals. For the "Vision" of Mother Ann Lee came to her in a Manchester jail after demonstrations of her religious fervor brought penalty of thirty days' imprisonment for disturbing the peace. It was not her first offense — nor the first time she had been put behind the bars of a British prison.

Ann Lee was a product of the dim environment of a mid-eighteenth-century English industrial city. She lived in squalor and observed the misery of kindred souls confined to a hopeless existence of poverty and constant suffering. Deprived of any formal education — she could neither read nor write — she had been cast into the maelstrom of hard labor in a textile mill while still a child. She was married, apparently against her will, on January 5, 1762, to Abraham Standerin, a loutish Manchester blacksmith. In rapid succession, during the next few years, four children were born of the marriage — all of whom died in infancy. It is understandable that her involuntary participation and sordid experiences in matrimony engendered deep feelings of revulsion — and this undoubtedly prescribed the practice of celibacy as a prime tenet of the religion she later established.

The evangelical proclivities of Ann Lee first came to light when she joined a Quaker couple, the Wardleys, in divine worship. The Wardleys and their few followers were not conventional Quakers. They had come under the influence of the French Prophets, or Camisards, who were driven from France because of the emotional disturbances their unorthodox preachings caused among the people.

The Camisards prophesied the early return of God's kingdom to earth — an idea which did not sit too well with the current French king. When the French government put a stop to their activities, some escaped to England, where they were known as "The Prophets." But their preachments were too fanatical for export. In England their numbers dwindled to extinction — and it was not until the start of the religious revivals of the mid-eighteenth century that their prophecies were remembered.

It was during the era of religious awakening that James and Jane Wardley corroborated the Camisards' testimony by announcing that the Second Coming of Christ was near at hand. Ann Lee, imbued with the conviction that God must have intended a better lot for miserable mankind than the bitter experiences of her own youthful years, eagerly joined the Wardleys in voicing the Words of the Prophets.

Because of her natural leadership, Ann soon took over the organization and administration of the new religious sect. Later they came to be known as "The United Society of Believers in Christ's Second Appearing." For short, they called themselves "The Believers" — and not until several years later, when the physical eccentricities of their religious ritual was ridiculed by the "outside world," were they dubbed "Shakers."

While most of the revivalist movements of the "Era of Awakening" were fanatical, Ann Lee was also practical in her spiritual fervor. In her search for God, she sought reasons why mankind behaved so badly. Her own miserable experiences had engendered the conviction that man's undisciplined yielding to greed, pride, and sex caused most of his misery. Sex, in her opinion, was the worst offender.

Thus, she concluded, the conquest of self was infinitely more difficult than the conquest of nations. And she was convinced that absolute self-denial would bring Paradise back to Earth. On the basis of these beliefs she enunciated the four fundamental principles of the Shakers' faith: confession of sins; community of goods; celibacy; and withdrawal from the sinful world.

Obviously, these renunciations of the flesh and the odious ways of the world did not popularize the Believers with their less enlightened neighbors. Indeed, their utopian beliefs and their noisy meetings that sometimes lasted long into the night — and their conversions of the citizenry, which often resulted in breaking up families — caused rumblings of suspicion which flared up into mob reprisal. The Believers, like the Quakers, abhorred physical violence and their faith prevented them from returning the blows of their adversaries. Thus, time and again, members of the little sect were unmercifully beaten and imprisoned either on the complaint of their neighbors, who unjustly accused them of starting the trouble, or because the authorities deemed it wise to confine them for their own protection.

The Vision of Ann Lee

It was during one of her stays in the Manchester jail that Ann Lee received the "Vision" which certified that her place was parallel to that of Jesus as Christ's Second Emissary. Her "Vision" transported her to the lap of God, where it was revealed that she was the anointed successor of Jesus — the incarnation of the Word of God again to be given to man in this Second Coming of Christ. She was *Ann the Word* — and would henceforth be known as "Mother Ann."

As reports spread of Ann Lee's "Vision," membership in the Society commenced to grow. People were starving for spiritual solace and many burdened souls were brightened in Mother Ann's radiant presence. She comforted them and instructed them in gentle tones on the simple steps of self-denial which would guarantee their salvation. Thus, the select group increased its membership.

But growth of membership also produced greater dangers in their relations with the outside world. The Believers were constantly under attack. They were stoned and whipped, and even Mother Ann herself was subjected to torture — with attempts made to take her life. Her relationship with the Deity would not let her admit of any actual suffering. (Jesus, too, she rationalized, had been stoned and whipped and suffered to carry His cross to Calvary.) But at length the persecutions became so severe that converts, in self-protection, had to abandon the faith.

It was then that Mother Ann had another "Vision." This time she was enjoined by the Almighty to take her most loyal followers to America.

As in all her undertakings, blind faith in divine providence again paved the way. For Ann Lee's penniless sect did have two moneyed members — John Townley and John Hocknell — and they eagerly financed the trip. Thus on May 10, 1774, Mother Ann Lee and her eight followers departed from England to build God's empire in the New World.

The American Adventure

Arriving as strangers in New York on August 6, 1774, the little band had to separate and seek individual employment. But Mother Ann assured them that this condition was only temporary and that soon they would settle in their own community away from the "outside world." And, as usual, her word was as good as the deed.

Shortly thereafter they learned that a tract of "cheap land" was available at Niskeyuna (now Watervliet, New York), about eight miles northwest of Albany. One of their financial benefactors, John Hocknell, accompanied by Ann's brother, William Lee, and James Whittaker went up the Hudson River to investigate. The land, although swampy, seemed suitable. So it was purchased with Hocknell's money, and under Whittaker's supervision work was begun on the first American Settlement.

In 1779, the Shakers' first house was built at Niskeyuna, only to burn to the ground shortly after its completion. Another cabin was built, however, and Mother Ann and her little family — all of

Second Meeting House, at New Lebanon, New York, was built in 1824. It was here the Shakers provided special benches so that visitors from the "outside world" could witness their spirited religious rituals. *Photo courtesy Index of American Design, Washington, D.C.*

whom were totally inexperienced at farming — moved in and started to plant their crops. While their isolated home in the wilderness was not located advantageously for attracting converts to the Society, Ann's gift of prophecy again assured her followers that the faith would surely spread. "They will come to us like doves," she announced. Actually, they didn't have long to wait.

The Converts Come Over

The Believers' obscure cabin at Niskeyuna gained notice during the "Great Awakening" of religious fervor which started in New England during the mid-eighteenth century. (As in England, the Shakers invariably advanced during periods of religious revival.)

One such revival erupted in June 1779 among the New Light Baptists in the neighboring towns of New Lebanon in New York and Hancock in Massachusetts. The leaders of the movement were Joseph Meacham, a lay preacher from Enfield, Connecticut, and the Reverend Samuel Johnson, who had been first pastor of the Presbyterian church in New Lebanon.

There had been revival meetings all summer long in the barn of George Darrow, a prosperous farmer of New Lebanon. Here they held nightly gatherings during which the preachers thundered dire warnings of hell and damnation which whipped their listeners into frenzied pleas for salvation. Visions, signs, and prophetic utterances were followed by hysterical shouting and screaming, which often terminated with the fainting and falling of men and women "as if slain in battle." All were convinced that the triumphant "Second Coming of Christ" was close at hand. But as the summer waned and Christ failed to appear, the enthusiasm of the revivalists commenced to vanish.

Exhausted by their emotional exertions, and largely disenchanted, the revivalists started to return to their homes. Tramping through the woods on their way back, two of them stumbled upon Mother Ann's little "family" at Niskeyuna. Here they were greeted and fed as though their visit had long been expected.

Impressed by the sanctity and obvious sincerity of Mother Ann — and conditioned by the recent revival to expect the Second Coming of Christ — the visitors promptly returned to New Lebanon and reported their discovery to the leaders of the revival. On receiving the news, Joseph Meacham decided to make his own appraisal of this mysterious "woman of the new birth."

Meacham had chosen an auspicious day for his meeting with Mother Ann. While the story may be apocryphal, it was reported that this was the famous "dark day" of May 10, 1780, when "the sun disappeared from the sky with neither clouds nor smoke in sight." People all over New England were panic-stricken by the phenomenon. They gathered in groups to gaze at the heavens, howling and wringing their hands and chanting in terror, "The Day of Judgment is come." According to legend, it was on this day and under these weird circumstances that the first public opening of the testimony was held at Niskeyuna.

The visitors from New Lebanon were deeply moved by what they heard and saw. They spoke of miracles, gifts of healing, mysterious signs, and singular rituals. That Ann Lee was a woman, apparently endowed with supernatural powers, roused the curiosity even of those who were not religiously inclined. Soon the small log house at Niskeyuna which served as both church and dwelling was crowded with visitors. And they continued to arrive for the next two months not "like doves" as Mother Ann had predicted but in droves so large that the prophetess and her family exhausted their spare provisions trying to feed them. But with characteristic hospitality, the Shakers did their best to make the visitors comfortable — and they sent them back to their own homes strongly indoctrinated in the Shaker faith.

During the next few years groups of Shaker converts met in private homes at New Lebanon, and Hancock. Then the Word spread throughout New England. Proselyting efforts of Mother Ann and her little Niskeyuna group were augmented by the new American converts who traveled afar to start branches of the faith at Enfield, Connecticut; Canterbury, New Hampshire; Tyringham, Massachusetts; Alfred, Maine; Enfield, New Hampshire; Harvard and Shirley, Massachusetts; and New Gloucester (Sabbathday Lake), Maine. The first of these groups was the Society at New Lebanon, where the first Shaker meeting house was completed on September 8, 1784.

American Persecutions

As in England, when the word started to spread and membership began to increase, the "outside world" took unfriendly notice. So, as the faith continued to grow, a reign of terror, even more cruel than the persecutions of Manchester, was again inflicted on the peace-loving Shakers. At first the "world's people" in America regarded this queer sect with contemptuous amusement. But soon their jeers and catcalls changed to violence.

To start with, the townspeople of New Lebanon resented Ann Lee's easy conversion of their two ministers — Baptist Joseph Meacham and Presbyterian Samuel Johnson. They also resented the manner in which the Shakers would enter a community and break up families in their recruitment of converts. To add fuel to their antagonistic fury, it was observed that the original Shakers came from England — with which the American colonies were then at war. Thus the slander was spread among their Yankee tormentors that they had been sent here as "English spies."

Persecutions increased in intensity wherever the Shakers appeared. On a trip undertaken by Mother Ann and the elders, between Niskeyuna and Harvard, Massachusetts, hostile mobs met them at every town along the way. They were constantly beaten and were often jailed on trumped-up charges. But the spirit of Mother Ann prevailed undaunted throughout this period of torture — and despite hostile opposition she and her disciples continued to spread the faith throughout New England. But there is no doubt that the hardships and physical injuries she sustained during her missionary travels contributed to Ann Lee's early death on September 8, 1784. Her brother William, his skull fractured by an angry mob, had died too, only a few weeks before the passing of Mother Ann.

The Perpetuation of Mother Ann's Work

Even by those who discounted her divine pretensions, Mother Ann Lee was respected as a singularly gifted woman. Having voiced premonitions that her life in America would be brief (she died ten years after her arrival), she had instructed only the ablest men and women to carry on with her work. Her first apostle was James Whittaker. James shared Ann's "Vision" of the founding of the Church of Christ in America. Endowed with gifts of wisdom and leadership and the ability to preach the Word and convert others to his beliefs, Father James became the head of the church immediately after Ann Lee's death.

Joseph Meacham, born in Enfield, Connecticut, on February 22, 1741, was, before his conversion to Mother Ann's faith, a forceful preacher of the New Light Baptist Church at New Lebanon, New York. He was a man of considerable ability. Father Joseph served in second place as counsel and mentor to Father James Whittaker until Whittaker's death in 1787, when he became the first American-born leader of the Society.

Gathering in Gospel Order

When Father James Whittaker began his ministry, the Believers were living in scattered private homes. But both Whittaker and Meacham were intent on having them live together so they could withdraw from the hostile "outside world" and become entirely self-sufficient and self-supporting. The first such Shaker community to be gathered in "Gospel Order" was at New Lebanon in 1787.

All Shaker societies were organized into "Family" branches. Usually one 'Family' occupied a complex of buildings. Supreme authority was

TheTree of Life is sometimes regarded as the symbolic emblem of the Shaker religion. Actually, it originated as an inspirational drawing indicating, perhaps, the productive unity and beauty of the Believers' communal life. The original of this print, rendered in color, is believed to have been painted on July 3, 1854, by Sister Hannah Cohoon.

vested in the central ministry at New Lebanon. This was originally headed by Father Joseph Meacham and Mother Lucy Wright, but was later made up of two elders and two eldresses. The central ministry appointed the branch ministries of the other societies. Like large corporations today, it was all one organization, with many branches but one central headquarters from which policies and orders were issued.

Each "Family" of Shakers was governed in all things, spiritual and temporal, by the eldership, which, in turn, received its orders from the central ministry. But the temporal affairs of each "Family" were the direct responsibility of the deacons or trustees, of which there were two of each sex. They obtained their instructions from the elders.

Following the establishment of the first Shaker community at New Lebanon, communal dwellings were built at other places where the Believers hitherto had lived apart or in the houses of their more affluent members.

In the development of all these communities the administration of the central ministry played a vital part. Like Mother Ann, who had endured persecution in her travels to widely separated places — and who had so diligently sown the seeds which later blossomed into full-bloom Shaker communities — Father Joseph Meacham and Mother Lucy Wright, with their entourage of elders and eldresses, made constant visits to the outlying communities, directing and advising them on the conduct of their affairs.

The Shakers' Way of Living

As Shaker communities in eastern New York and New England were gathered into "Gospel Order," with buildings erected to house their "Families," a definite pattern of work and devotion was established. Primarily these were *working* communities. For Mother Ann's advocacy of "hands to work and hearts to God" was strictly observed — and all members, even to the smallest children, were usefully occupied at all times except during periods of worship. As will be noted, not only did the Shakers engage in many industries, and work hard at pro-

ducing superior products, but they also regarded work as a form of worship. Their inventive acumen and appetite for work contributed substantially to the improvement of any occupation in which they engaged.

During the pioneer period, when husbands and wives, together with their children, gave themselves over to Shakerism, their wholehearted acceptance of Mother Ann's rules was so sincere that few restrictions were required to maintain separation of the sexes. But as new converts flocked to the faith — many of them seeking economic security as well as spiritual solace — the elders deemed it necessary to set up detailed rules and regulations for governing the behavior and daily routine of all Believers. These rules were published in the early Shaker covenants and were later covered in minute detail in the "Millennial Laws" published in 1845.

To facilitate implementation of the basic rule requiring strict separation of sexes, even the buildings were especially designed so that brothers and sisters of the faith could live together in separate but equal status. For as well as having separate doors, stairways and apartments, other provisions were made to keep the men and women apart. At mealtimes they ate in the same dining room but at separate tables. All conversations between brothers and sisters were carefully chaperoned. Even the elders and eldresses were required to have a third adult present during their meetings.

Daily Routine

The Shakers' day started at four-thirty a.m. in the summer and an hour later during the winter months. They slept several to a room in dormitories — the sisters occupying one half of the house and the brothers the other. Rising at the sound of the morning bell, they knelt momentarily in silent prayer and then got promptly dressed and started their daily chores. But before leaving their rooms they stripped the covers from their beds and opened wide the windows, for their house rules advocated the advantages of fresh air and adequate ventilation.

Contemporary print shows Shaker sisters occupied in finishing room, cutting and stamping materials. While work kept the Shakers constantly busy, it progressed at an easy pace in efficiently organized rooms. *Old print courtesy the Andrews Memorial Shaker Collection, Winterthur Museum Libraries.*

FINISHING ROOM.

Social meetings of Shaker brethren and sisters sometimes took place during early evening hours. Seated five feet apart, male and female members sang hymns, discussed mutual working problems, or engaged in light conversation. *Old print courtesy the Andrews Memorial Shaker Collection, Winterthur Museum Libraries.*

Shaker Spirit Drawings gave artistic expression to visions of spiritual grandeur. Their imagery depicted mystical symbols, religious paeans, and "gifts" of God's blessings. *Early print courtesy Index of American Design, Washington, D.C.*

After they left their rooms, the sisters in charge of housework came in and made up the beds and swept and dusted the rooms. In the meanwhile, other sisters were busy in the kitchen preparing breakfast, while the brothers attended to their morning chores of bringing in the firewood, feeding the stock, milking the cows, or getting an early start on their shop tasks. Breakfast came an hour and a half after rising.

Shaker food was plain, wholesome, and plentiful. Fruits, vegetables, and dairy products came in abundance from their own farms, as well as meats of the livestock which they raised. The Shaker sisters took humble pride in "setting a good table" — and many of their recipes were sought after by the "outside world" and are even contained in cookbooks published today.

After breakfast, the sisters went on with their housework. They rotated their tasks to allow time for sewing, preserving, butter and cheese making, and numerous other domestic duties. They also engaged in industrial pursuits of weaving, basket making, tailoring, and other "female arts and crafts."

Among their many other virtues, the Shaker sisters were immaculate housekeepers. Mother Ann had admonished that dirt was the devil's doing and it must be relentlessly eradicated. The houses were purposely designed and furnished to facilitate cleaning. There were no moldings, ornaments, or bric-a-brac to collect dust. All rugs and fabrics were washable. Chairs and other items of the sparsely furnished rooms could be hung on pegboards — out of the way when the room was being cleaned. Indeed, the old adage "Cleanliness is next to Godliness" may have been Mother Ann's.

Following the morning meal, the brothers returned to their shops, mills, pastures, gardens, and

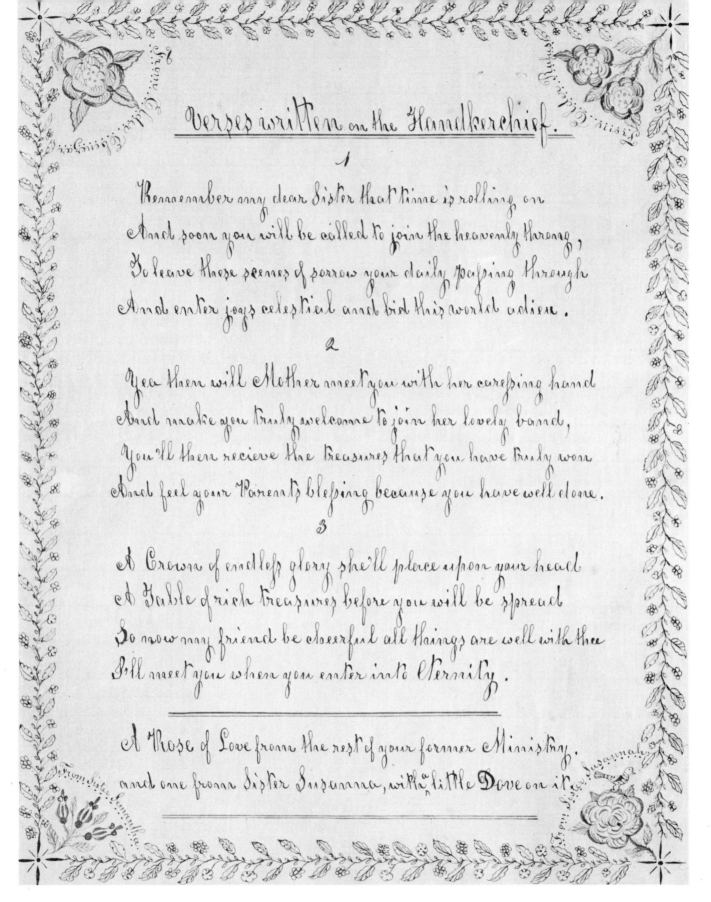

Verses written on the Handkerchief.

1

Remember my dear Sister that time is rolling on
And soon you will be called to join the heavenly throng,
To leave these scenes of sorrow your daily passing through
And enter joys celestial and bid this world adieu.

2

Yea then will Mother meet you with her caressing hand
And make you truly welcome to join her lovely band,
You'll then recieve the treasures that you have truly won
And feel your Parents blessing because you have well done.

3

A Crown of endless glory she'll place upon your head
A Table of rich treasures before you will be spread
So now my friend be cheerful all things are well with thee
I'll meet you when you enter into Eternity.

A Rose of Love from the rest of your former Ministry.
and one from Sister Susanna, with a little Dove on it.

Gifts of poetry were exchanged between Believers. Rendered in fine script, with embellished borders and symbols, the verses usually described heavenly raptures awaiting the recipient. *Print courtesy Index of American Design, Washington, D.C.*

11

orchards to perform their many works. Even the elders engaged in manual work. Father James Whittaker had been a weaver and was highly skilled in other trades. Job Bishop, elder of the Canterbury Shakers, was also a chairmaker. John Vance of Alfred, Maine, was a tailor, and Richard McNemar, besides being a distinguished writer, was also a printer and bookbinder and a cabinet-maker.

Since all forms of manual work were regarded as being especially blessed by the Almighty, the Shakers endeavored to do their work to perfection. Mother Ann had admonished them: "Do all your work as though you had a thousand years to live, and as you would if you knew you must die tomorrow."

It should be noted that despite the edicts of celibacy, there were always some children in the Shaker communities. At first they came when entire families were converted to the faith. Others came through adoption when mothers and fathers could no longer take care of them. They were free to leave the community when they arrived at adult age — but many preferred to stay. While living in the Shaker's care, they were well housed and fed and provision was made for their education.

As well as taking good care of the children, the Shakers were charitably inclined to look after anybody who came to them for help. Mendicants, regardless of faith, condition, or origin, were provided with free food and lodging and allowed to go on their way without any religious obligation. Their reputation for charitable hospitality became so widely known that they had to set aside rooms and guest houses to take care of the transients. Indeed, their hospitality was often abused by "winter Shakers" who came to them expressing a desire to join the faith, after the work of gathering the crops had been completed in the fall, and then hopped off the premises just before planting season in the spring.

But to get back to the Shakers' daily routine: At noontime the meetinghouse bell again called them to dinner. After the main midday meal they returned to a long afternoon of work. The formal ending of the day's labor came at six p.m. when the brothers and sisters were called to supper. In summertime, many returned to work while the twilight lasted. Bedtime was at nine or nine-thirty.

To relieve the daily monotony, some evenings were given over to "social" meetings — often of religious character. Sometimes the gatherings would become more animated with singing and marching or "laboring" when the Believers "labored to get good" by singing and dancing. Occasionally three or more sisters were allowed to visit with an equal number of brothers for songs and conversation. They sat facing each other in rows five feet apart and were permitted to converse on mutual work problems or on the less controversial news of the "outside world."

The Shakers' Way of Worship

But for the Shakers, Sunday was a day apart when all the restraints of the week were cast aside. For this was their day of worship — a day on which they seemed to vent off all the steam pent up during the week of disciplined labor. The incongruity of sober, orderly and industrious individuals, so completely cutting loose in the guise of worship, defies explanation. For once their Sunday ceremonies started, all inhibitions of their everyday lives seemed to escape in wild outbursts of song and dance with overtones of the mystical fanaticism which was part of their religious worship.

While, later on, the Shaker dances and rituals were rehearsed and became more formalized, the fanatical nature of their worship was laced with hallucigenic apparitions and a sort of spiritualism which seemed to induce mass hysteria. They joined in emotional outbursts of prayer for salvation and violent denunciations of the devil who lurked in the "outside world." They exhibited their "gifts" of song and movement as well as the "gift of tongues" which enabled them to sing in unknown languages and conduct mumbled conversations with St. Peter, John the Baptist, Mother Ann, and even General George Washington. All in all it was quite a show — and one which fully qualified their designation as "Shakers."

Missions to the West

During the last years of her life, when Shakerism was starting to take root in the New England

SHAKERS near LEBANON,
State of NEW YORK.

As part of their worship, Shaker sisters and brethren, dressed in their Sunday best, literally "shook" in ecstasy while singing and lifting their hands in rhythmic response to the dance ritual. Sometimes visitors from the the world outside were invited to witness their performance. *Early print courtesy the Andrews Memorial Shaker Collection, Winterthur Museum Libraries.*

communities, Mother Ann Lee had prophesied that the opening of the gospel would soon spread to states of the southwest. Thus it was with particular interest that the ministry at New Lebanon learned of the strange religious upheaval which started in Kentucky near the turn of the century. This had all the earmarks of the New Lebanon Revival. But it was more widespread and revolutionary than the movement which had started the Shakers in the east.

Between the years 1800 and 1805 the "Western Awakening" had spread into Kentucky, Ohio, Indiana, and Tennessee. Always alert to the opportunities which revivals provided for planting the faith, and remembering Mother Ann's prophecy, the New Lebanon ministry decided to send emissaries to the southwestern states.

On January 1, 1805, John Meacham (elder son of Father Joseph), Benjamin Youngs, and Issachar Bates started on foot on their western journey. With one horse to carry their luggage, they trudged along the stage routes through New York, Philadelphia, Baltimore, Washington, and on to Lexington, Kentucky. Outside of Lexington they visited sites of the various revivals.

On March 9, 1805, they crossed the river into Ohio, where they attended other meetings. Here they met and visited at the home of Malcolm Worley at Turtle Creek near Lebanon in Warren County, Ohio. At this terminus, Issachar Bates wrote: "We have found the first rest for the soles of our feet, having travelled 1,233 miles in two months and twenty-two days."

The Presbyterians first sponsored the western camp meetings in 1799, hoping to revive the spiritual life of their frontier communities. This set off a chain reaction with other churches competing to capture converts.

13

RING DANCE, NISKEYUNA

The Shaker "Ring Dance" was performed in intricate circles, within circles, with members moving their hands to "gather blessings" and stamping their feet to "tread out evil." Meanwhile they chanted songs or shouted "Love, Love!" in staccato chorus. *Early print courtesy the Andrews Memorial Shaker Collection, Winterthur Museum Libraries.*

For five years the "Great Revival" gained momentum. Conservative leaders of the established churches, who had started the movement, never expected anything like this. The religious hysteria was contagious. People came by the thousands "on foot, on horseback, in wagons and other carriages." And the meetings went on continuously for nights and days at a time.

It was in this climate of upheaval that the three New Lebanon missionaries found the fields well plowed for planting the seeds of Shakerism. Their first contact, Malcolm Worley, with whom they had visited at Turtle Creek, Ohio, was impressed by their demeanor and their spiritual message. He invited some of the revival preachers, including Richard McNemar and Burton Stone, to his home to meet the missionaries. Within the following week Worley accepted their message, and shortly thereafter — when the Shakers cured one of his children of an ailment he had suffered since birth — McNemar regarded the "miraculous cure" as a

long-awaited "sign" and eagerly accepted the Shaker teachings.

Following the conversion of these two stalwarts of the revival, the Shaker missionaries were enthusiastically received on all sides. And after their preachings, conversions followed in rapid order.

As the word spread, there was such widespread demand to hear the Shakers preach that the three "Prophets from the East" had to separate and go from place to place individually so that crowds at the many revivalist camp meetings could hear them. On both sides of the Ohio River, people came from hundreds of miles away. Indeed, their work increased to such an extent that in July the New Lebanon ministry sent out three more missionaries, including David Darrow, who later became the head of the first Shaker community in the west, at Turtle Creek, Ohio.

By September the indefatigable Issachar Bates, realizing that Shakerism was really "taking hold," walked back to New Lebanon to raise funds for the

SHAKERS AT MEETING. THE RELIGIOUS DANCE

Whirling in ecstasy, Shaker sisters would revolve and twist in one spot, meanwhile chanting and muttering in mystical "tongues." Often this would be followed by "falling into trances," after which they would recite divine messages from Mother Ann and biblical characters. *Early print courtesy the Andrews Memorial Shaker Collection, Winterthur Museum Libraries.*

Final procession of the Shaker Sunday worship. Sisters and brethren solemnly leave the meeting hall, their hands uplifted bearing the "gifts" bestowed during their hours of strenuous devotion. *Early print courtesy the Andrews Memorial Shaker Collection, Winterthur Museum Libraries.*

SHAKERS AT MEETING. THE FINAL PROCESSION

purchase of land at Turtle Creek. (The Shakers later renamed this "Union Village.") Returning with the money, he and his cohorts immediately set to work building a large house, into which the first western community gathered in 1806. In June of that year, two more brothers and seven sisters of the New Lebanon community joined the new establishment at Union Village.

During the next few years the Believers multiplied throughout the southwestern area. Issachar Bates, "the relentless proselytizer," made repeated journeys through Ohio, Kentucky, Indiana, and Illinois. Often he went alone, but sometimes in the company of Richard McNemar, Benjamin Youngs, Malcolm Worley, Matthew Houston, and others.

Persecution patterns of the past again assailed the Shakers wherever they started to settle. Angry mobs burned down their houses and committed cruel violence against individual members and groups. Agitators of the angry mobs were usually defectors or disgruntled preachers of other faiths.

The people of Lebanon, Ohio, were particularly hostile toward the Shakers — while the residents of Cincinnati seemed to adopt a more benign attitude. Hence the Shakers of Union Village (near Lebanon) decided to place a seldom invoked Shaker "curse" on the town of Lebanon while, simultaneously, "blessing" Cincinnati. This was performed with full ritual — and the effectiveness of the performance may be judged by the fact that immediately thereafter Cincinnati expanded and prospered while Lebanon, at least until recently, remained a small country town. Once again, that old Shaker magic seemed to work!

Soon the societies in Ohio and Kentucky were gathered into "Gospel Order" with each community containing its own families of Shakers. Union Village in Ohio was the parent ministry of the southwestern Shaker colonies. Here David Darrow (transplanted from New Lebanon) was assisted by Richard McNemar in administering the rules of living, both spiritual and temporal — subject to the overall guidance of the central ministry at New Lebanon, New York. Watervliet was the second Ohio community to be gathered. In Kentucky, there were two communities: South Union, which was gathered in 1811, and Pleasant Hill, in 1814.

An abortive attempt was made to colonize a wilderness community at Busro in the Indiana Territory. The community was gathered in 1810 and for a short while all seemed to go well. But Indian attacks, combined with raids of renegade soldiers during the war of 1812, caused the entire community to move back to the Shaker settlements in Kentucky and Ohio for the duration of the war. They returned to Busro after hostilities ceased. But the swampy climate induced an epidemic of malaria which killed off most of the members. The survivors then decided that the combined hazards of the wilderness and its lethal climate were too much to bear. So, in 1827, they closed the community forever and walked back to join the more fortunate Believers in Kentucky and Ohio settlements.

This, in substance, marked the end of Shaker colonization. Only three other communities were gathered in later years. These were: Whitewater, Ohio (near Cincinnati), in 1824; North Union, Ohio (now Shaker Heights, near Cleveland), in 1826, and Groveland, New York, which was gathered at Sodus Point in 1826 and later moved to Sonea. While many attempts at Shaker colonization were made thereafter (including abortive attempts in Florida and Georgia), there were no new colonies gathered in "Gospel Order" after 1826.

Shaker Industries

The only thing that rivaled the Shakers' dedication to God was their appetite for hard work. Since they regarded work as worship, they actually expressed their devotion to the Almighty by the many labors they performed. Ann Lee and her Manchester followers were working people — many of them skilled artisans. Their converts in America were of similar abilities — and the application of their many trades made the Shaker communities not only self-supporting but productive of profitable goods with which they engaged in commerce with the "outside world."

Fundamentally, they were fine planners and organizers and in most instances astute businessmen. They selected the sites of their communities with careful consideration of the fertility of the land, its

The Shakers are credited with starting the garden-seed industry in this country. In 1790, the Watervliet Shakers sold seeds to neighboring farmers, thus launching a commercial enterprise which spread to other communities. Their invention of a "printing box" enabled them to make their own seed labels. *Photographed by author at the Shaker Museum, Old Chatham, N.Y.*

Special "broom corn," cultivated by the Shakers, was used in their invention of the first *flat* brooms, at Watervliet, New York, during the 1790's. Thereafter, demand for the improved flat brooms created another flourishing Shaker industry. Photo shows special clamps designed by the Shakers to facilitate flat-broom production. *Photographed by author at the Shaker Museum, Old Chatham, N.Y.*

Shaker production of butter and cheese was increased with specially designed cradle churn, shown above with tub churn and other dairy accessories. *Photographed by author at Hancock Shaker Village, Hancock, Mass.*

Production of assorted types, sizes, and shapes of wooden buckets, basins, bins, tubs, and baskets was another industry in which the Shakers excelled. *Photographed by author at Hancock Shaker Village, Hancock, Mass.*

The Shaker cooperage shop at Old Chatham displays original tools and barrels made with pre-bent staves. These could be "knocked-down" for flat stowage and were used in the West Indian molasses trade. *Photographed by author at the Shaker Museum, Old Chatham, N.Y.*

proximity to ample water supply and to woodlands for building materials, and adequate drainage to ensure a healthful climate. Hence all the Shaker places, east and west, were located in beautiful parts of the country — as may be observed by those who visit these sites today.

As early as 1790, Joseph Turner, who maintained the family garden at Watervliet, New York, offered surplus seeds for sale. Because these were superior seeds, they were eagerly bought by neighboring farmers. In fact, the demand soon became so great that seed production was increased and special species were cultivated. Henceforth, each planting season was heralded by appearance of the "Shaker seedmen" who went to the farmers with their wagons loaded with the season's supply. This led to a substantial business. It even necessitated calling the sisters from their domestic duties, each season, to help at sewing seed bags. It also caused the invention of a "printing box" to speed production of seed-bag labels. The success of the Watervliet seed enterprise soon spread to other Shaker communities, east and west, and opened the doors of commerce for the marketing of other Shaker products.

It was a short step from the marketing of seeds to the collection and cultivation of herbs for medicinal uses. These were compounded into the famous "Shaker remedies" — powders, ointments, tonics, and patent medicines — which were widely used in America and exported abroad. The Shakers were gifted healers, and although their religion frowned on the "world's Medicine" (they called upon doctors only in extreme emergencies), the many medications concocted of their own herbs had the reputation of effecting miraculous cures.

It is probable that the Shakers' love of cleanliness led them, at an early date, to despair of the deficiencies of the makeshift round brooms which were commonly used at that time. Thus, as early as 1791, they started to cultivate a species of corn which provided stronger and more resilient bristles. Having developed their "broom corn" they went one better by inventing a clamp device with which the bristles could be pressed flat and bound to form the first flat brooms — the type we use today. Soon the Shakers' flat brooms, first made at Watervliet,

Large loom in the Sister's Weaving Room, at Hancock Shaker Village, produced assorted fabrics for community use as well as some varieties which were sold outside. *Photographed by Louis H. Frohman at Hancock Shaker Village, Hancock, Mass.*

Shaker shoes were made on this rugged old cobbler's bench which is now displayed at the Shaker Museum in Old Chatham. Spinning wheel, yarn reels, and weaving accessories are shown in background. *Photo courtesy Index of American Design, Washington, D.C.*

This huge pulley wheel was used to transmit power to the Shaker sawmill at Mt. Lebanon, New York, before 1845. Water wheels, on nearby streams, provided source power that was conveyed by pulley wheels and shafts to the shop machinery. *Photographed by author at the Shaker Museum, Old Chatham, N.Y.*

New York, were sought after by every housewife in the country, and this started a separate broom-making business, which again carried to other communities.

Ultimately, the ramifications of Shaker industries represented a fair cross-section of all things done and made in America during the first half of the nineteenth century. But the Shakers, through their inventions, introduced new industries, and because of their dedication to superior workmanship, they did things better.

The welcome the world now extended to their enterprise encouraged further developments. Because of their landholdings, they were primarily agriculturists, and they endeavored to extract the ultimate of what their land could produce. Quite early they started to engage in selective breeding of livestock. Soon superior breeds of "Shaker cattle" were bought by neighboring farmers to freshen their stock. Toward the middle of the nine-

teenth century the community at Union Village, Ohio, became so famous for its fine strains that it started exporting blooded Durham stock to Europe.

They raised Merino sheep and wove the wool into the renowned "Shaker flannels." Dairy products and preserves were put up by the Shaker sisters not only to feed their own communities but to sell to a waiting world market. Their orchards were carefully cultivated to yield better fruits. At South Union, Kentucky, mulberry trees were introduced to sustain silk worms with which they produced the beautiful "Shaker silks" that were soon widely in demand.

Because the Shakers operated as a united society, with complete exchange and interchangeability of knowledge and skills between all communities, east and west, they had practical advantages and a financial stability which were not common to isolated farmers and small businessmen of the world outside.

Frequently one community functioned best at producing a certain thing. South Union, Kentucky, for example, excelled in the production of silk. But whenever possible the product developments of one community would be passed along and shared with the others. Also, if one or more of the members possessed special knowledges and skills at doing a certain thing, they were "loaned" to other communities to instruct them in their specialties.

Shaker Shopwork

As already noted, the Shakers were ingenious artisans. The list of their shop pursuits is almost endless, including such occupations as tanning, weaving, tailoring, printing, bookbinding, cabinetmaking, basketry, stonework, brickmaking, patternmaking, fabrication of felt, metalwork, blacksmithing, and wire-drawing. They were also clockmakers, tinkers, and makers of hollow-ware, plows, hoes, rakes, clothiers' shears, and most other tools, machines, and implements used for their work.

Above all, wood was the favorite working material. Since the sites of Shaker settlements had been prudently selected for their proximity to both woodlands and water, they did not want for building materials, nor for the power to extract lumber from the virgin forest.

Thus, with settlement of a new community, the Shakers' first concern was to erect water-powered sawmills and then similarly powered gristmills and fulling mills. The machinery of these mills was usually powered by water turbines (of their own invention) located along their streams.

As the production from their shops and mills increased, the Shakers found ready outlets for their merchandise in the towns and cities of their regions. Many storekeepers were proud to stock the superior Shaker wares, and the income derived therefrom made most Shaker communities of the early and mid-nineteenth century independently wealthy. However, since their faith did not approve the accrual of worldly wealth, they applied their profits only to the advancement and betterment of their communities, or to the charitable alleviation of their less fortunate neighbors.

Foundry patterns, precisely crafted of wood, were made by the Shakers for casting machine parts and objects of iron and other metals. *Photo courtesy Index of American Design, Washington, D.C.*

Hand-wrought door pulls, latches, and other metal accessories are so neatly designed and detailed that they seem to refute the Shakers' disdain of deliberate artistry. But the designs of Shaker master metalworkers were fundamentally functional. *Photograph above courtesy New York State Museum, Albany, N.Y.; photograph below courtesy Index of American Design, Washington, D.C.*

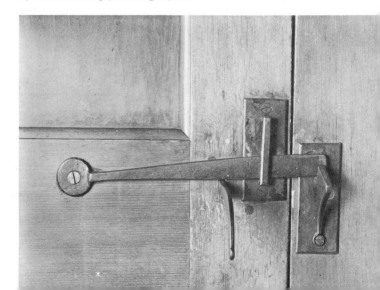

21

Chair-tipping device was invented by the Shakers to prevent slipping and protect floors when chair was tilted back to slanted seating position. *Photo courtesy New York State Museum, Albany, N.Y.*

Flat broom clamps, invented by the Shakers, were made in assorted sizes for binding large and small brooms. *Photo courtesy New York State Historical Museum, Albany, N.Y.*

Electrostatic machine was invented in 1810 by Brother Thomas Corbett of Canterbury, New Hampshire. While believed to have electrotherapeutic value, it proved principles later applied by Thomas Edison. *Photo courtesy Index of American Design, Washington, D.C.*

The first circular saw blade was invented in 1810 by Sister Tabitha Babbitt of the Harvard Shakers. *Photographed by Lees Studio at the Shaker Museum, Old Chatham, N.Y.*

Despite the mysticism of their beliefs, the Shakers were usually astute businessmen. The organization and administration of their shop industries would do credit to a latter-day Henry Ford or the board of directors of General Motors. All of their dwellings, shops, and mills were kept in top repair, and only the best of materials and tools were used for construction. If new and more efficient tools and machinery were developed outside their community, they promptly purchased the improved items — even going so far as to import hand tools from England. And they constantly sought new ways to increase production with less manual labor. Thus, from the time of their arrival in America, they distinguished themselves as prolific inventors of time-saving machines and devices.

As time went by, Shaker peddlers, their horse-drawn wagons loaded with Shaker wares, became a familiar sight along the country roads. And they were greeted as welcome visitors at the towns and farms throughout New England and the southwest states. No longer were they persecuted like their pioneering predecessors; they were hailed as long-awaited friends who came bearing "gifts" of fine merchandise which their outside neighbors were eager to buy. For the American Shakers, while still regarded as a bit queer in the practice of their religious rituals, were universally respected for the quality of their goods.

Transom ventilators, of Shaker design, were installed above dormitory doors at Hancock. The Shakers were ardent advocates of fresh air and adequate ventilation. *Photo courtesy Index of American Design, Washington, D.C.*

Shaker Inventions

Aside from being superb craftsmen, the Shakers were also the leading inventors of their time. Unfortunately, they have never been given full credit for all the things they did invent — since they seldom took patents, believing that all useful things should be shared with the world. Their ability to invent was stimulated by the climate of their communal life. Living and working together, they shared each other's problems. And when any particular problem relating to their work arose, they discussed it at communal meetings. Then the best brains of the community, often augmented by the thinking of other communities, concentrated on providing a practical solution. In most instances their solutions came in the form of inventions which, like the flat broom, served to do the job more quickly and efficiently.

In their domestic mileau they were constantly improving their systems of lighting, ventilating, heating, refrigeration, and laundering. Shaker buildings, standing today, are remarkably light and airy and exhibit features of design and construction far in advance of other buildings erected during that era.

Having devised a system to pipe water into their buildings from elevated aqueducts, the Shakers at Canterbury, New Hampshire, added a water-powered cooling fan, with faucet attached for drawing fresh water. The carved table appears too elaborate for Shaker design. *Photo courtesy Shelburne Museum, Inc., Shelburne, Vt.*

Shaker experiments in development of an efficient washing machine began early in the nineteenth century and resulted in their patenting of the "Improved Washing Machine," in 1877. This was awarded the Gold Medal at the Philadelphia Centennial Exhibition. Left section of the improved machine is shown below. *Photo by Lees Studio, courtesy the Shaker Museum, Old Chatham, N.Y.*

SHAKER EAST. This handsome brick dwelling was built by the Shakers at Hancock, Massachusetts, in 1830. At one time it housed 100 Shakers. With its many bright and spacious rooms, furnished as they were during Shaker occupancy, this building forms part of the Hancock Shaker Village complex — a National Historic Landmark, which is open to visitors during the summer months. *Photo courtesy Hancock Shaker Village, Hancock, Mass.*

They were always eager to experiment with something new, and both male and female members participated in solving each other's working problems. As an example, the first circular saw was not invented, as would be supposed, by a woodworker, but by a Shaker sister — Tabitha Babbitt of the Harvard community — who, while watching her spinning wheel, pondered that a revolving water-powered blade could saw planks at speeds infinitely faster than gangs of men laboriously operating hand saws. Thus her invention of the circular saw revolutionized lumber processing and the same principle led to subsequent invention of a tongue-and-groove machine, planers, and other cutting apparatus which utilized revolving power.

Aside from flat brooms, circular saws, and washing machines, the Shakers are believed to have invented the common clothespin, therapeutic static electric machine (1810), water-powered cooling fan, chair tilters, the side-hill plow, sash-balance counterweights, filling machines (for herb packaging), Babbitt metal, improved heat-circulating stoves, methods of utilizing compressed air, stick pins, cut nails, condensed milk, screw propellers, rotary harrows, threshing machines, pea shellers, silk-reeling machines, improved windmills, fertilizer spreaders, apple parer and corer, revolving ovens, bed rollers, and screw-fed lathes. They are also credited with invention of metal pens, door ventilators, lumber-drying kilns, and numerous other innovations which were first used in their own communities and then altruistically shared with the world.

Prosperity

During the first half of the nineteenth century, and right up until the start of the Civil War, the Shakers continued to grow and prosper. The third decade of the century saw them settled in eighteen communities, with fifty-eight families scattered from Maine to southwest Kentucky, numbering as many as 6,000 members between 1840 and 1860.

At the summit of their growth, New Lebanon, New York (which was renamed "Mt. Lebanon" after 1861), and Union Village, Ohio, led the societies with about 600 members apiece. Pleasant Hill, Kentucky, was next with 500. Watervliet, New York; South Union, Kentucky; Enfield and Canterbury, New Hampshire; and Hancock, Massachusetts, each had approximately 300 members. The remaining ten communities averaged around 200 members each.

The lands and buildings they owned were valued at millions of dollars. In all they had acquired some 50,000 acres of choice real estate located in the most picturesque parts of the seven states in which they settled.

All Shaker lands were put to most effective use. The communities buzzed like beehives, ever busy with their many activities. Prized breeds of livestock grazed in lush pastures. Vegetable gardens, fruit orchards, and acreage planted with grain, corn and oats kept their granaries, barns, cellars, and pantries amply stocked. From adjoining woodlands came building materials as well as the wild berries, herbs, and maple syrup which they extracted and preserved. In Kentucky, the mulberry trees they had introduced eventually produced a thriving silk industry.

Shaker cotton mills in Massachusetts; woolen mills in New Hampshire; and in all the communities, seed, herb, broom, cooperage, cabinetmaking shops; tanneries, forges, stone and brickworks; print and tailoring shops; and many other enterprises — all flourished. They were housed in substantial buildings of brick, stone, or wood, erected in scientifically planned communes. Each family had its own occupations and was virtually self-supporting.

In 1841, the Church Family of Enfield, New Hampshire, erected the famous Shaker Mills for the weaving of flannel. Ultimately this led into big business, with the mills doing thousands of dollars of trade with the "outside world." Similar

SHAKER WEST. Center House, at South Union, Kentucky, was completed in 1824. The resemblance between Shaker architecture east and west may be noted by comparing this Kentucky brick building with the one at Hancock, Massachusetts, shown on opposite page. *Photo courtesy Shaker Museum, Inc., Auburn, Ky.*

The round stone barn, at Hancock, Massachusetts, was built in 1826. Even by present-day standards, it is regarded as a marvel of functional architecture. It could accommodate 52 head of cattle, with stalls ingeniously arranged below a central hay mow and with working access from three levels. Completely restored in 1968, the barn is still studied by agriculturists and architects from all over the world as an outstanding example of efficient design. *Photographed by author at Hancock Shaker Village, Hancock, Mass.*

ventures introduced large industrial sawmills, gristmills, and public-works developments, which contributed not only to the commerce of the Shakers but also to the industrial enrichment of towns and cities in regions where they lived.

The Decline

Unfortunately, the Shakers mounting interest in worldly commerce ran contrary to the early rules of the United Society — and their ambitions to amplify their industrial output may have contributed to their decline. Certainly, their increased exposure to the world was bound to erode the spiritual values which held them together. For while their religious doctrine enjoined them to avoid worldly competition, they were obliged to compete with the world's merchants in order to achieve success.

Life in the Shaker communes, while providing abundantly for body comforts, economic security, and spiritual solace, was necessarily restrictive of individual freedom and initiative. Thus, as early as the 1820's, younger members in the Ohio and Kentucky families started to show signs of discontent. Fewer people joined the society, and each year more and more members abandoned the faith.

During the ten years before the Civil War the increase in Shaker defections became alarming. As their membership started to shrink the signs became unmistakably clear that American Shakerism had reached its zenith and was now on a downhill path which would lead to its ultimate extinction.

Along with other causes it is obvious, too, that the Shaker rule of celibacy was a built-in instrument of extinction. They could not produce their own progeny to perpetuate the faith. Most of the children who came to them with proselytized parents, and the foundlings for whom they cared, left them when they arrived at adult age.

To add to their woes, a series of misfortunes occurred during and after the Civil War which damaged their situation still more. The Civil War put

The Hancock Laundry and Machine Shop building was erected, in part, in 1790. Its basement contains the Shaker-built turbine which furnished power for the machines on the floor above. It also houses the laundry and seed and herb shops. *Photographed by author at Hancock Shaker Village, Hancock, Mass.*

The Church Family dwelling at Enfield, New Hampshire, built by the Shakers in 1837, is now occupied by a religious order. Its massive construction of smooth granite blocks would warrant continued use for centuries in the future. *Photographed by author at Enfield, N.H.*

Sister Sarah Collins, of the Hancock community, braids the seat of a Shaker chair. With termination of their chair-making enterprise at Mt. Lebanon, New York, the Shaker sisters continued to assemble, weave, and finish chairs until their communities finally closed. *Photo courtesy Index of American Design, Washington, D.C.*

to test the Shakers' principles of nonviolence and vehement conscientious objection to wars of any cause. The Shakers refused to be drafted into armies North or South. The locations of their communities in Ohio and southern Kentucky placed them in the path of both belligerents. They were cleared of obligation to bear arms by no less a personage than Abraham Lincoln, who listened to their petitioners and granted them immunity from combat.

But President Lincoln's tolerant understanding did not deliver the Shakers from the hardships of war. Indeed, the communities of Pleasant Hill and South Union, Kentucky, were torn between occupying forces of both the Union and the Confederacy. The noncombant Shakers cared for the sick, wounded, and hungry of both sides. Despite their impartial mercies, their lands were ravaged by marauding armies with losses of buildings, livestock, and equipment to the extent of more than one hundred thousand dollars. The war losses were never recouped.

But it was not just the destruction of property and loss of money which caused Shaker membership to dimish. During and after the Civil War a

contagion of discontent infected the members. America was now moving ahead, and what the Shakers saw outside their isolated communes now looked much brighter than it had during the beginning years of the nineteenth century. Moreover, the Shakers were essentially agriculturists and hand craftsmen, and the arrival of the Industrial Age brought factories and mass-manufacturing techniques with which their simple provincial industries could no longer compete.

Thus, by the 1870's, the total Shaker membership dwindled from 6,000 to 2,500. A decade later, and rapidly thereafter, entire communities, or parts of communities, were closed. By the turn of the century, whole Shaker societies had been discontinued.

Even the New Lebanon, New York, society, which had housed the central ministry, had to sell most of its land and buildings in 1933. The Church Family buildings were sold to a boys' school, which was appropriately named the Darrow School to honor George Darrow, the pioneering Shaker on whose farmsite the first Shaker Church was built.

Shortly thereafter, in 1960, the few members still living at Hancock, Massachusetts, sold their properties. Fortunately, the Hancock Shaker Village, as it is now known, was kept intact by a historical society. This lovely tract of land, with its picturesque buildings, including a world-famous Shaker round barn, now attracts thousands of visitors.

As this account is being written only the communities at New Gloucester (Sabbathday Lake), Maine, and Canterbury, New Hampshire, remain in Shaker hands. Here the few remaining Shaker sisters (the last Shaker brother died in 1961) are as busy as their sisters of a century ago — only now their most important industry is that of tourism. With quiet dignity they show visitors around their properties and through their buildings, pointing out features of the dwellings, furniture, and artifacts with which their families lived more than a century and a half ago.

Paradoxically, as the sun sets on American Shakerism, the people of this country are suddenly becoming aware of the great force for good the Shakers were. And we are beginning to recognize, too, the enormous contributions the Shakers made to America's cultural and industrial development. As a token of belated recognition it is gratifying to observe that the United States Pavilion at the Japanese "Expo 70" World's Fair featured a display of Shaker furniture and craftwork as exemplary of the finest workmanship produced by the early industries of this country.

But perhaps the recognition the Shakers themselves would appreciate most is the simple inscription on a bronze tablet marking the Shaker Bridge at Enfield, New Hampshire.

SHAKER BRIDGE BUILT BY THE SHAKERS IN 1848. WAS DESTROYED BY HURRICANE IN 1938. REBUILT BY THE STATE HIGHWAY DEPARTMENT IN 1940. DEDICATED TO THE SHAKERS FOR THEIR MANY SERVICES TO THE TOWN OF ENFIELD, N. H. TRULY INDUSTRIOUS — ALWAYS HELPFUL — A KINDLY PEOPLE.

SHAKER GHOST TOWN. As Shaker communities closed, buildings were abandoned and many of the wooden structures fell into disrepair. Fortunately, the sturdy stone and brick buildings suffered only superficial damage — and many of them have been preserved as historical landmarks. Most buildings at Mt. Lebanon (photographed below, a few years after the Shakers left) have now been restored and are being used as a boys' school. *Photo courtesy Index of American Design, Washington, D.C.*

SUMMARY OF SHAKER SETTLEMENTS

LOCATION	YEAR OF ORIGIN	MAXIMUM NUMBER FAMILIES	APPROXIMATE PEAK MEMBERSHIP	SHAKER OCCUPANCY TERMINATED
New York State:				
WATERVLIET (Niskeyuna)	1787	4	350	1938
MT. LEBANON (New Lebanon)	1787	8	600	1947
GROVELAND (Originally at Sodus Point)	1826	2	200	1895
Massachusetts:				
HANCOCK	1790	3	300	1960
HARVARD	1791	4	200	1919
TYRINGHAM	1792	3	100	1875
SHIRLEY	1793	3	150	1909
Connecticut:				
ENFIELD	1792	5	200	1917
New Hampshire:				
CANTERBURY	1792	3	300	
ENFIELD	1793	3	350	1923
Maine:				
ALFRED	1793	3	200	1932
NEW GLOUCESTER (Sabbathday Lake)	1794	3	150	
Ohio:				
UNION VILLAGE (Turtle Creek)	1806	6	600	1910
NORTH UNION (Shaker Heights)	1822	3	200	1889
WHITEWATER	1824	3	150	1907
WATERVLIET (Beulah)	1813	2	100	1910
Indiana:				
WEST UNION (Busro)	1810	2	200	1827
Kentucky:				
SOUTH UNION	1811	4	350	1922
PLEASANT HILL	1814	8	500	1910

CHAPTER II

SHAKER FURNITURE DESIGN

Austere, but adequate, furnishing of Shakers' rooms is evident in this reassembly of typical furniture. Drop-leaf table came from the South Family of Watervliet, New York. The armed rocker is an early Hancock design. Both the tripod table and drop-leaf chest are believed to be early products of New Lebanon, New York. The three-step stool and looking glass are of Hancock origin. All pieces originally of the Andrews Collection. *Photo courtesy the American Museum in Britain.*

Shaker Furniture Design

Of their many industries, inventions, and communal endeavors, the Shakers have come to be best known for their fine furniture. Their utilitarian concepts of furniture design placed them at least a century ahead of the Bauhaus school of functionalism. The purity of the Shaker style is followed even today by leading contemporary designers.

Shaker furniture is, above all, functional. It works and it serves. In strict adherence to practical principles, it discards all adornments of decorative embellishment which do not contribute to basic requirements. Whatever beauty it attains — and most Shaker designs are beautiful — was not produced by deliberately striving for beauty. Rather, it came as a by-product of the Shakers' dedication to fine craftsmanship in endeavoring to create something perfect unto its purpose.

For the Shakers believed perfection was attainable in their temporal as well as their spiritual endeavors. They also regarded work as an important form of worship. To quote from their own writings regarding performance of work, they contended: "Anything may, with strict propriety, be called perfect which perfectly answers the purpose for which it was designed. A circle may be called a perfect circle when it is perfectly round; an apple may be called perfect when it is perfectly sound."

Since a perfectly useful piece of furniture must first be sound and strong, the Shakers started with this premise and then went on to consider all other aspects of its function. This involved study of exactly how the furniture would be used; the people who would use it; the most appropriate materials for its construction; the proper dimensioning of its parts; and its absolute adaptability to the environment of its use.

Shaker craftsmen were free to experiment. Except for a few models of their commercial output which appeared in later years, they were not confined to the making of standardized types and sizes of furniture. As the designs shown on these pages indicate, a wide variety of ideas, based on specific needs, allowed ample leeway for the craftsman to create furniture of assorted dimensions and descriptions. Many pieces were designed to meet the needs of individuals as well as their communal environment.

Shaker inventiveness also contributed to the design of original types of chairs, chests, desks, work tables, and other items. Many of these were custom-built for their particular functions.

Since many pieces of Shaker furniture were designed for communal use in the large buildings which housed the many societies, functions of such furniture differed from that designed for small family dwellings. Dining tables were extended in length to accommodate many members at mealtimes. Benches and settees were stretched for multiple seating. Work tables and desks were often fashioned with separate drawers and counters, accessible on both sides and ends, so two or more people could work together. Huge chests of drawers with top cupboards and entire walls of built-in cupboards, drawers, and compartments were designed to serve the Shakers' strict sense of neatness and orderliness by providing "a place for everything and everything in its place."

Despite their versatility, it should be noted that when Shaker craftsmen created what they regarded as a perfectly useful design, they often retained that design for an indefinite period thereafter. Some of the classic Shaker chairs and rockers first made during the early years of the nineteenth century remained only slightly modified in their final production almost a century later.

Furniture Making:
An Early Shaker Industry

As early as 1789, Shaker craftsmen started building furniture at New Lebanon, New York. In this community, as in all others, membership was made up in part of skilled artisans. Many of them had worked as furniture makers before they joined the Shakers.

The original Shaker craftsmen followed the traditional, solid-wood designs which had originated in this country during the seventeenth and eighteenth centuries. But the restrictions of the Shaker religion applied to their work as well as their worship. Thus, in his "way marks," written during the seventeen-nineties, Father Joseph Meacham laid down the following rules for the performance of work:

"All work done, or things made in the Church for their own use ought to be faithfully and well done, but plain and without superfluity. All things ought to be made according to their order and use; and all things kept decent and in good order according to their order and use....

"We are not called to .... be like the world; but to excel them in order, union and peace, and in good works — works that are truly virtuous and useful to man in this life."

In their adherence to Father Joseph's principles of avoiding superfluity, Shaker craftsmen departed from their colonial colleagues by designing furniture devoid of elaborate scrollwork and ornamental turning. Such embellishments they regarded as "worldly show." Instead they made their furniture perfectly plain. But they whittled their work down to perfect proportions and introduced functional features seldom found in the colonial furniture of early America.

At the start of the nineteenth century when American cabinetmakers were turning to the more sophisticated mahogany furniture of Chippendale and Hepplewhite, involving intricate inlays, veneers, carving, and upholstery, the Shakers divorced their designs from any association with such ornate trends. Instead they retained and refined the solid-wood patterns of previous centuries — adding their own improvements to create a style uniquely "Shaker."

During the decades following their start at New Lebanon, furniture construction — particularly the making of chairs — went along with the successful seed and herb business to become an important element of Shaker industry. Recognizing the superiority of their products, people were eager to buy Shaker furniture, with the result that more and more communities turned to furniture making as a source of income. Several societies originated salable designs which were commonly followed by craftsmen of other communities east and west.

It will be observed, however, that there were some slight differences between the designs of eastern and western Shaker furniture. The eastern product often tended to be more austere than that of the west. Craftsmen of the Ohio and Kentucky communities, many of whom had migrated from Virginia and other southern states, were naturally influenced by regional cultures of the places from which they came. Hence, many of their furniture designs were of heavier construction and sometimes yielded to mild embellishment of scrollwork and other decorative details frowned on by their brethren of the east.

Woods, too, were different. While in New York and New England, pine, maple, birch, ash, cherry, hickory, and butternut were commonly used, in the west, walnut, cherry, beech, and poplar seemed to be more abundantly available. By and large, however, the edicts of New Lebanon were followed in all areas — and in some instances it is difficult to determine regional origins of certain Shaker designs.

Despite regional touches of individuality, the "pure and simple" lines of Shaker furniture identified a style which continued to be made and sold right up until termination of Elder Robert Wagan's chair business in the 1930's. Thus the era of fine Shaker craftsmanship, which had continued at New Lebanon, New York, for over a century, came to a close when the few remaining Shaker sisters were no longer able to continue the work.

The wide assortment of types and sizes of Shaker furniture may be observed with the variety of work tables, chairs, rocker, and stand which are displayed in the Sisters' sewing shop at Hancock. *Photographed by author at Hancock Shaker Village, Hancock, Mass.*

The Shakers' improved stove dominates the sparse furnishing of this typical dormitory. Wood box, drop-leaf table, rocker, and candlestand are all early products of the New York and New England Shaker communities. Side chair hangs from pegboard in typical Shaker fashion. All furniture originally of the Andrews Collection. *Photo courtesy the American Museum in Britain.*

Chairs and rockers of many descriptions were beautifully built by Shaker craftsmen. Designs were widely varied, as were the materials of their construction. Infant's high chair and children's rockers shown here were made at Mt. Lebanon, New York, during the final decades of the nineteenth century. The miniature rockers adhere to the same details of design as the larger models. *Photographed by author at Hancock Shaker Village, Hancock, Mass.*

Shaker Chairs

Of the many types of furniture they produced, the Shakers were most prolific in their manufacture of chairs and rockers. Chair makers of the New Lebanon community started building their own distinctive designs, for sale to outside markets, during the 1790's — and their business continued well into the twentieth century. (It was, in fact, their final shop industry.) While the world outside their communities might know little about the Shakers, people everywhere were well acquainted with Shaker chairs. Thus the profitable chair-making enterprise, which started at New Lebanon, soon spread to enrich the coffers of other Shaker communities in the east and west.

Shaker chairs gave positive expression to the religious craftsman's aspiration to produce something perfect unto its purpose. Unlike most other chairs made during their era, they were light and strong and adroitly adapted to support the human body in a comfortable seated position. While they were made in many types and sizes — from the smallest children's chairs to the tall, ladder-back classics — they all possessed the virtues of being superbly made and beautifully suited to requirements.

The chairs best known and most widely sold by the Shakers were the so-called "slat-backs," which were made with bent back slats and delicately turned legs with round or pointed finials. These were usually made of maple, sometimes of the curly or birds-eye variety. Ash and hickory, as well as maple, were used for the rungs. Construction of these chairs demonstrated the diligence of Shaker craftsmen in whittling off excess weight without impairing the strength and durability of their workmanship.

The back slats were usually planed to precisely 5/16″ thickness, with an ever-so-slight graduation in the widths of each successive slat. Legs and back posts were mildly tapered at the ends. The purpose, apparently, was to remove useless wood. But, esthetically, it gave the chair a light and delicate appearance which seemed to belie the considerable strength of its construction.

In contrast to the tall ladder-back was the Shaker's low-back dining chair of similar construction. This was made with one or two curved slats, with the back posts shortened so that it could be tucked under the table after mealtime.

Other Shaker chairs were made of variable heights and sizes, either to adapt them to physical requirements of individuals, or to fit them for certain types of work. A variety of small, solid-wood, pegged chairs ("sewing chairs") were made in many communities either for children or for adult tasks which could be best performed in a low seated position.

Most Shaker chairs had caned or woven seats. At first they were woven with narrow hickory splint. But after 1830, cane, rush, colorful worsted tapes, and other materials were used. Near the middle of the century the Shakers invented their tilting-chair device, which was inserted under the tips of the back legs to prevent slipping or marring of floors when the chair was tilted back against a wall.

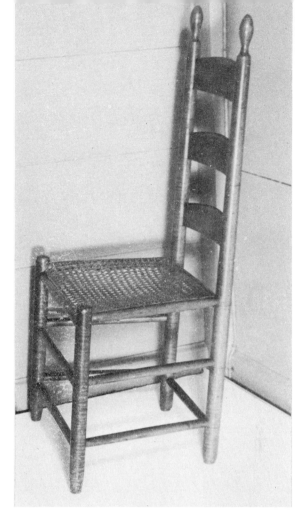

Light weight and delicate proportions of this maple chair, which was made at the Harvard Shaker community around 1850, belie its obvious edurance and strength. *Photographed by author at Fruitlands Museums, Harvard, Mass.*

This low-back, rush-seated dining chair is believed to have been built at Hancock, Massachusetts, around 1830. *Photo courtesy the Henry Ford Museum, Dearborn, Mich.*

An interesting assortment of small, wooden chairs, seldom of duplicate design, were made by Shaker craftsmen of the many communities. *Photographed by author at the Canterbury Shaker Museum, Canterbury, N.H.*

"Revolvers," as the Shakers called them, were made in New York and New England communities as early as 1830. *Photo courtesy New York State Museum, Albany, N.Y.*

Pedestal based "revolvers" were widely used as sewing chairs and as piano stools. *Photographed by author at the Shaker Museum, Old Chatham, N.Y.*

Another distinctive chair of Shaker invention caused some confusion when the curator of one of the museums was examining old inventories of Shaker furniture. Time and again the inventory sheets made reference to "revolvers." Knowing that the peace-loving Shakers would have no use for such weapons, the curator's curiosity continued until it dawned upon him that what they really meant was *revolving chairs.*

Shaker revolving chairs and swivel stools were produced in abundance and in a variety of sizes and styles. They were widely in demand for use with sewing machines and were also used as piano stools. Taller models were used by accountants and as bank-tellers' stools.

Shaker Rockers

While they can't be credited with "inventing" the rocking chair, the Shakers did more to develop its design and promote its use than any other chair-makers. At first, Shaker rockers were designed to bring comfort to the aged and infirm. But since their religion held no scruples against comfortable seating, they soon made rockers for standard furnishing of their communal dormitories. Then, of course, the world outside their communities be-

This unusual "ironing chair" with bent slat-back and protruding step was made at South Union, Kentucky, around 1830. *Photographed by author at the Shaker Museum, Auburn, Ky.*

came aware that the Shakers had developed something better, with the result that Shaker workshops in all communities were kept constantly busy turning out rockers for the popular market.

From the very start of their production at New Lebanon, which dated back to the last decade of the eighteenth century, the Shakers demonstrated unique acumen at fashioning fine rocking chairs. At first they were rather slim and severe in appearance. But after 1830 their modifications of size and structure caused them to be regarded as the most comfortable seating designs made in America.

The exceptional comfort of Shaker rockers did not happen by accident. Every component of their structure was carefully measured and fitted to suit the human body. Nowadays this science is understood by contemporary chair designers. But more than one hundred and fifty years ago, Shaker craftsmen in their search for functional perfection experimented with proportions in relation to physical requirements until they hit upon just the right balance of parts.

Shaker rockers were designed with or without arms. The most popular models had scrolled arms with "mushroom" post turnings to top off protru-

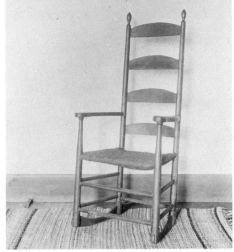

Early Shaker rockers were slim, trim, and severe. This model was made around 1830. *Photo courtesy New York State Museum, Albany, N.Y.*

Armless rockers were made in many Shaker communities. *Photo courtesy Index of American Design, Washington, D.C.*

Advertising cuts, of a nineteenth-century catalog, indicate range of sizes and prices of "R. M. Wagan & Co." Shaker slat-back rockers. This company of Shakers made chairs and rockers for the wholesale trade at Mt. Lebanon, New York, from the mid-nineteenth century until the community closed during the 1920's. *Catalog print courtesy the Shaker Museum, Old Chatham, N.Y.*

The Shakers' Slat Back Chairs, with Arms and Rockers.

WORSTED LACE SEATS.

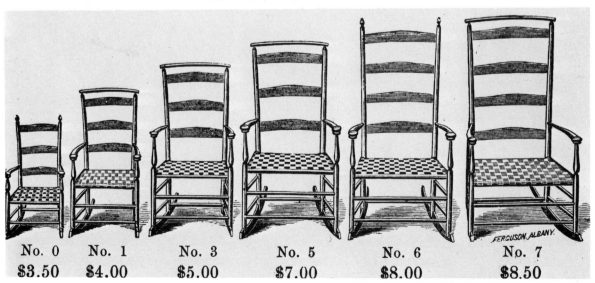

No. 0	No. 1	No. 3	No. 5	No. 6	No. 7
$3.50	$4.00	$5.00	$7.00	$8.00	$8.50

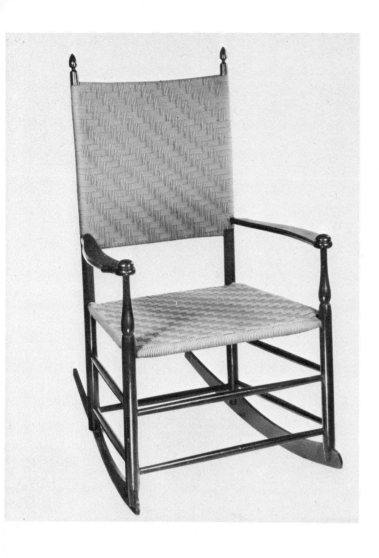

This handsome rocker, which was made by the Wagan Company at Mt. Lebanon, New York, sometime after 1860, shows the fine details and harmony of proportions which made Shaker rockers so popular. Worsted tape, which was used for weaving the back and seat, came in many bright colors and was often woven in contrasting checkerboard patterns. These rockers were finished with natural stain and varnish, or in lustrous ebony. Below is a miniature copy made for children. *Photo at left courtesy the Henry Ford Museum, Dearborn, Mich.*

sions of the front leg tenons. They were made in graduated sizes, starting with diminutive children's rockers — little gems of craftsmanship — and ranging up to the "great" rockers of full adult size. As well as being constructed with slat backs, many were made with dowel framed backs which were woven with panels of colored braid.

Seats of the early slat-backs were woven of narrow hickory splint as well as straw "rush." But in later models, worsted braid (called "listing") was woven in contrasting colors and patterns (often checkerboard patterns), thus adding a bright new note to the designs. Some were made with top rungs instead of finials on the back, for attaching cushions — or, as they were called, "upholstery mats."

Shortly after 1850, the Shaker chairmakers of New Lebanon became engaged in mass production of chairs and rockers. Later, under the leadership of Elder Robert Wagan, their industry was formally organized and advertised under the name

The armless, slat-back rocker (below) is believed to have been made at Mt. Lebanon, New York, around 1860. *Photo courtesy the Henry Ford Museum, Dearborn, Mich.*

Harmonious combination of Shaker rocker and pedestal table represents two periods: the cherry table was made around 1830 and the chair sometime after mid-nineteenth century. *Photo courtesy Index of American Design, Washington, D.C.*

This earlier design of Shaker slat-back rocker was made at New Lebanon, New York, around 1850. *Photo courtesy the Henry Ford Museum, Dearborn, Mich.*

Shaker slat-back rocker and sewing stand were made at Hancock, Massachusetts, around the middle of the nineteenth century. *Photo courtesy Index of American Design, Washington, D.C.*

This unorthodox bentwood Shaker rocker is believed to have been made at Mt. Lebanon, New York. *Photo courtesy Index of American Design, Washington, D.C.*

of R. M. Wagan & Co. Manned by Shaker craftsmen, the Wagan Company accepted wholesale chair and rocker orders from mail-order houses and department stores in the principal cities. They published catalogs, which were often inscribed with religious aphorisms as well as illustrations and descriptions of Shaker chairs and related items of furniture.

In one of their early catalogs, the Wagan chairmakers declared: "Our chairs offer the advantages of durability, simplicity and lightness." Fairly said! Another catalog noted: "Our largest chairs do not weigh over ten pounds, and the smallest weigh less than five pounds, and yet the largest person can feel safe in sitting down without fear of going through them." Apparently "going through them" was a common seating hazard of that era.

As a climax to popular acclaim for the virtues of Shaker chairs and rockers came the award they received when exhibited at the Philadelphia Centennial Exhibition in 1876. Here the Shaker products of R. M. Wagan & Co. were honored with a medal and diploma for their "Strength, Sprightliness and Modest Beauty."

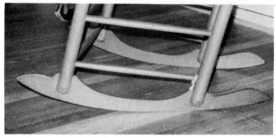

Unusual detailing of scrolled arms and rockers made this Union Village, Ohio, design particularly noteworthy. *Photographed by author at the Warren County Historical Museum, Lebanon, O.*

This combination of rocker and swivel chair seemed to stretch Shaker ingenuity. It was built by Brother Alonzo Hollister at New Lebanon in 1858. *Photo courtesy Index of American Design, Washington, D.C.*

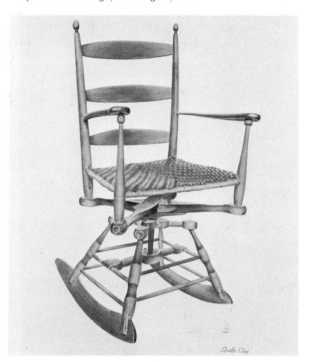

Chair lifters — called "boots" — were made by South Union, Kentucky, Shakers around 1830. *Photographed by author at the Shaker Museum, Auburn, Ky.*

42

Benches and Settees

Along with their chairs and rockers the Shakers devoted much time to exploring the design possibilities of elongated seating pieces. Many different types were developed. Most notable, perhaps, was the so-called "Canterbury Bench" which may or may not have originated in that community — Harvard has also been credited with its origin. In any case, this meetinghouse bench, designed with multiple tapered spindles supporting a shaped back rest, was made in many New England communities as early as 1855. Because of its delicate shaping and fine proportioning of parts, it is surprisingly comfortable — even though the seat is made of a solid wooden slab.

Numerous other designs of benches and settees were built in Shaker workshops of the east and west. Most of these were of original concept and exhibited qualities of lightness and buoyancy rarely found in the more massive benches built at that time by manufacturers outside the Shaker communities.

This perky settee, made of maple and ash, is believed to have been built at Canterbury, New Hampshire, around 1880. *Photographed by author at the Shaker Museum, Old Chatham, N.Y.*

Meeting-house benches, of the type illustrated below, were built at Canterbury, New Hampshire, between 1855 and 1865. This design was also made in many other Shaker communities. *Photo courtesy the Henry Ford Museum, Dearborn, Mich.*

This handsome turned trestle table was built at Hancock, Massachusetts, before 1840. The low-back dining chairs, circa 1830, came from Watervliet, New York. *Photographed by author at the Shaker Museum, Old Chatham, N.Y.*

The earliest Shaker trestle tables had square, chamfered posts and plain feet, slightly concave at the bottom. Top rail was tenoned through the posts. Table and chairs, above, date around 1830. They came from Hancock, Massachusetts. *Photo courtesy New York State Museum, Albany, N.Y.*

Solid walnut trestle table was made at South Union, Kentucky, circa 1850. Boards forming the top are joined horizontally across the table instead of spanning the length. *Photograph courtesy the Shaker Museum, Auburn, Ky.*

Shaker Tables

Although Shaker tables were sometimes sold outside the communities, for the most part they were designed for use by the Shakers themselves. Thus there was very little standardization of types and sizes as would be required if they were quantity-produced. Instead they were made in an assortment of sizes and styles with many designs apparently custom-built for a particular purpose.

Large tables of the trestle type, designed for communal dining, were made in many models. Shaker trestle tables differed in construction from those of early American design. Those made in this country before the Shakers arrived were heavily built, with a center rail spanning midway down the leg posts. Shaker craftsmen eliminated the excessive weight and connected their center rails up underneath the top where it would not obstruct the legs and knees of those seated at the table.

Shaker trestle tables measured upward to twenty feet in length — although the usual top dimensions were approximately ten feet by three feet. Shorter models were made for the two elders and two eldresses, who sat together at mealtimes. The earliest trestles were plainly built with chamfered posts and flat, tapered feet. Later the feet were arched (probably to allow toe room at the ends) and the posts were either scroll-shaped or turned.

Although pine was most frequently used for the tops, a variety of other woods, including ash, oak, maple, cherry, and walnut, were used for other parts. Some of the ministry tables were made entirely of cherry or walnut. Walnut was most frequently used in the western Shaker communities.

Among other tables of Shaker design the assortment seems almost limitless. However, there were only two types of legs: some were square and tapered, others were made plain and turned. Tables came in all shapes and sizes, ranging from the little bedside stands with delicately turned legs to the huge types already described..

Following their practice of eliminating all excess weight, the light tables (which the Shakers sometimes called "nice") were precisely proportioned with all parts shaved down to minimum thickness.

Shorter length of this trestle table suggests it was made for the Shaker Ministry. An unusual feature is its metal angle bracing of legs. This cherry table was made at Shirley, Massachusetts, circa 1840. *Photographed by author at Hancock Shaker Village, Hancock, Mass.*

This trestle table was used by the Ministry of the Church Family at Hancock, Massachusetts, about 1830. Two Shaker elders and two eldresses sat apart, at tables like this, in a small room adjoining the common dining hall. *Photo courtesy Index of American Design, Washington, D.C.*

Drop-leaf sewing tables, made by the Shakers at Hancock, Massachusetts, early in the nineteenth century, were models of fine design and superb craftsmanship. *Photo courtesy Index of American Design, Washington, D.C.*

Elongated cherry work table, with drawers staggered on both sides, was made at New Lebanon, New York, circa 1850. *Photo courtesy the Henry Ford Museum, Dearborn, Mich.*

Many Shaker tables were designed to facilitate certain types of work. Sometimes the apron drawers were staggered on both sides and ends so that two or more members could work together around a single table. Others were more massively built for use as kitchen utility tables or for shop chores.

Apart from the trestle types and four-legged designs, the Shakers also specialized in the construction of single-standard pedestal tables. These, too, displayed exceptional individuality of style, and their assortment of sizes and types places them in a category of their own.

The "working" pedestals — or tripod stands, as they were sometimes called — were made with plain, chamfered standards and pegged legs. Others had simple, bulb-turned standards which were angle-bored near the bottom to receive turned peg legs. These utility pedestals were used for sorting seeds, for reading stands, for simple sewing stands, and for other purposes.

At the opposite extreme, of sophisticated design, were the beautifully styled Shaker pedestals with exquisitely turned stems and curved or undulating legs. These were made in the eastern colonies throughout the nineteenth century. In their free-flowing symmetry of shapes and proportions, some Shaker pedestals may be regarded as artistic masterpieces.

Delightful little Shaker tables were made of many different designs. This example is believed to have been built at New Lebanon, New York, circa 1840. *Photo courtesy the New York State Museum, Albany, N.Y.*

Southern Kentucky influence is reflected in the design of this cherry table made at South Union, circa 1850. *Photographed by Ray Pearson at Western Kentucky University Museum, Bowling, Ky.*

This sprightly cherry table was made at Canterbury, New Hampshire, early in the nineteenth century. *Photo courtesy the Henry Ford Museum, Dearborn, Mich.*

Small cherry table, with delicately tapered legs, was used by the North Family at New Lebanon, New York, around 1840. The Ithaca calendar clock is not a Shaker product, although the Shakers were prolific clock makers. *Photo courtesy the New York State Museum, Albany, N.Y.*

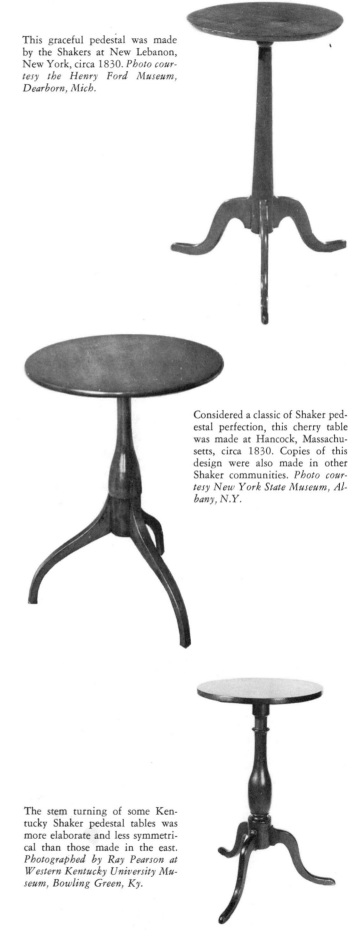

This graceful pedestal was made by the Shakers at New Lebanon, New York, circa 1830. *Photo courtesy the Henry Ford Museum, Dearborn, Mich.*

Considered a classic of Shaker pedestal perfection, this cherry table was made at Hancock, Massachusetts, circa 1830. Copies of this design were also made in other Shaker communities. *Photo courtesy New York State Museum, Albany, N.Y.*

The stem turning of some Kentucky Shaker pedestal tables was more elaborate and less symmetrical than those made in the east. *Photographed by Ray Pearson at Western Kentucky University Museum, Bowling Green, Ky.*

Between the primitive tripod stands and the perfected pedestals there appeared many modified models of utility tables based on single, turned stems. These were constructed with drawers attached beneath the tops. Uusually the drawers could be pulled out from both sides so that two Shaker sisters could pursue their tasks of sewing and knitting while seated on opposite sides of the table.

Stem-turning patterns of pedestal tables varied in the many communities. Usually the turnings were of unadorned, tapered, or symmetrical vase shapes. But the western pedestals sometimes yielded to the turning of decorative balls and rings — not unlike those of early American embellishment. In general, the western pedestals were more crudely turned and lacked the fine proportions of those made in the east.

While most pedestals were mounted on three legs, occasional models were made with cross-lapped, four-legged bases. The woods used in construction varied according to locality, with maple and cherry most frequently used in the east and walnut or cherry in the west.

Shaker Desks

Almost as varied as the tables were the many different designs of Shaker desks. The abundance of desks seems to refute an edict of the early church. For the Shaker leaders did not encourage the sisters and brethren to engage in personal writing. However, they themselves were incessant writers of journals and kept written records of practically everything that happened in their communities. So it is probable that most of the early desks were made for the exclusive use of the elders and eldresses of the ministry.

Several designs of small, portable desk boxes were made in the many communities. These were shaped either as square, oblong boxes, or with slanted lids which served as writing counters. They were neatly lined and constructed with compartments for ink pots, pens, and other writing equipment. Sometimes they were carried about as "traveling desks" to go with the Shaker elders and missionaries on their journeys to and from the outlying communities.

The slant-lidded desk boxes were enlarged and mounted on legs to form stationary desks. Some of these were beautifully constructed with delicately tapered legs — apparently as special gifts from the craftsman to favored elders or eldresses.

Slant-lid lap desk made at New Lebanon, New York, circa 1850. *Photographed by author at the Shaker Museum, Old Chatham, N.Y.*

Pine school desk made at Watervliet, New York, around 1880. *Photographed by author at the Shaker Museum, Old Chatham, N.Y.*

This pine desk was made at Canterbury, New Hampshire, in the mid-nineteenth century. *Photographed by author at the Shaker Museum, Old Chatham, N.Y.*

This delicate little Shaker desk is believed to have been made at Hancock, Massachusetts, around 1840. *Photo courtesy New York State Museum, Albany, N.Y.*

49

Utility desk-cupboard, of pumpkin pine, was built at Hancock, Massachusetts, circa 1830. It was probably used for keeping kitchen accounts. *Photographed by author at Hancock Shaker Village, Hancock, Mass.*

Early Shaker desk made at Sabbathday Lake, Maine, circa 1820. Variation of "revolver" chair has bent metal rods supporting the back. *Photographed by author at the Shaker Museum, Sabbathday Lake, Me.*

This walnut sewing desk was made for Sister Angeline Perryman of the South Union, Kentucky, Shakers, circa 1850. *Photograph by Ray Pearson, courtesy Western Kentucky University Museum, Bowling Green, Ky.*

(Many of the elders were also skilled cabinetmakers, so they may have made their own desks.) Since sizes were seldom standardized, it would appear that these desks were custom-built to fit the physical requirements of the individuals for whom they were made. Cruder forms of the slant-lidded design were constructed for use as school desks, and taller models were elevated on long legs, apparently to serve as accountants' desks.

Desk cupboards, fitted with shelved compartments and dropleaf counters, were designed to contain ledgers and housekeeping account books. These were installed in kitchens or workrooms where those in charge could make written records of domestic or shop transactions.

In the western communities Shaker desks often assumed a less orthodox appearance. Some of them were made with top galleries of spindle turnings. Others had scrolled counters and assorted ornamental fittings which were not strictly in keeping with the Shaker philosophy of perfectly plain and unadorned design. Most of these were used as "sewing desks" and were fitted with drawers and recessed racks for holding spools and other requirements.

Another design of South Union, Kentucky, sewing desk, circa 1860, was made of cherry. Ingenious spool drawer retracts flush when not in use. *Photo courtesy the Shaker Museum, Auburn, Ky.*

This pine sewing desk is believed to have been made at New Lebanon, New York, around 1850. *Photo courtesy the Henry Ford Museum, Dearborn, Mich.*

51

Two-drawer lidded chest of pumpkin pine was made at New Lebanon, New York, circa 1820. *Photographed by author at the Shaker Museum, Old Chatham, N.Y.*

Pine lidded chest with one drawer was made in an eastern Shaker community around the middle of the nineteenth century. *Photo courtesy the Henry Ford Museum, Dearborn, Mich.*

Pine chest of drawers was built by Elder Joseph Myrick of the Harvard Shakers in 1844. *Photographed by author at Fruitlands Museums, Harvard, Mass.*

This ponderous cherry chest of drawers was built at South Union, Kentucky, around 1860. *Photo courtesy Western Kentucky University Museum, Bowling Green, Ky.*

Shaker Chests and Cupboards

Living together in communal dwellings, the Shakers needed more case furniture — chests, cupboards, and built-in areas of drawers, cupboards, and storage closets — than the average householder. Order and neatness was a religious principle, in the practice of which the Shakers provided "a place for everything and everything in its place" by building ample storage facilities. Everything that was not in actual use was immediately put away in drawers or cupboards to avoid even the slightest intimation of clutter or untidiness.

A variety of small boxes were designed for the storage of special articles. Lidded blanket chests which graduated into lidded chests with one, two, or three drawers were specially constructed for storage of woolens and linens. Full chests of drawers of ample capacity were used for storage of clothing and personal belongings.

Shaker chests of drawers were designed for beauty as well as utility. Most of them were superbly proportioned with the drawer widths graduated — narrow at the top and wide at the bottom — to produce harmonious effects of lightness and fine balance. (Chests of drawers are among the few articles of Shaker furniture which were sometimes signed by the maker. Usually the signature of the craftsman is inscribed with date of origin beneath one of the drawer panels.) Taller chests, which required steps for access to

Pine wall cupboard was built by the Harvard, Massachusetts, Shakers around 1840. *Photographed by author at Fruitlands Museums, Harvard, Mass.*

Tall pine case of drawers was made by Massachusetts Shakers around 1850. *Photo courtesy the Henry Ford Museum, Dearborn, Mich.*

the top drawers, and massive chest-cupboards were shared by several members. Apparently separate drawers were assigned to each individual.

Sometimes the design of western Shaker chests of drawers became a bit "wordly" in the use of scrolled aprons and other mild forms of surface embellishment. One western chest, which was autographed by the craftsman, indicating that it was built at Union Village, Ohio, in 1827, bears remarkably close resemblance to a French Provincial design of the same era. More frequently, however, the western Shaker chests — particularly those built in southern Kentucky — are heavier and more ponderous than those made in the eastern communities.

Combinations of chests of drawers with top cupboards were used for general storage in working areas of the Shaker dwellings as well as in the dormitories. Despite their massive bulk, many of these are quite handsome. Obviously, the assorted "sets of steps," which the Shakers also designed, were needed to climb up to the top cupboards.

Large and small drawerless wall cupboards — beautifully built, with dovetailed corners and door frames through-tenoned and pegged — were made for various uses. These were attached to walls of kitchens and workrooms to store the tools and utensils of domestic pursuits.

Chest of drawers, with cupboard top, was built by the Harvard Shakers around 1840. *Photographed by author at Fruitlands Museums, Harvard, Mass.*

Case of drawers, with cupboards, was built at New Lebanon, New York. *Photographed by author at the Shaker Museum, Old Chatham, N.Y.*

Floor-to-ceiling built-in drawers and cupboards were installed in the walls of this Hancock Shaker community building. *Photo courtesy Index of American Design, Washington, D.C.*

Another wall at Hancock had 84 herb drawers, of graduating sizes, built in flush from floor to ceiling. *Photo courtesy Index of American Design, Washington, D.C.*

Shaker Built-ins

An entire book could be written on the ramifications of Shaker built-in furniture. Desire for the ultimate in neatness and orderliness undoubtedly influenced design of myriads of integrated components of drawers, cupboards, and compartments which occupied entire walls of many Shaker dwellings. Functional designers today, in their search for solutions to the everpresent problem of providing adequate household storage facilities, undoubtedly find answers by studying the schemes of organized wall storage which the Shakers designed more than a hundred and fifty years ago.

From wall to wall and from ceiling to floor the Shaker craftsmen patiently built their incredible complexes of drawers, closets, compartments, and cupboards. And despite the diversity of components involved, when the drawers were closed and the doors shut, the entire storage wall became a harmonious plane relieved only by the fine fitting of horizontal and vertical parts studded with carefully aligned rows of knobs and pegs.

As an example of how extensively the Shakers applied their built-in wall storage ideas, it may be noted that the Church Family dwelling at Enfield, New Hampshire, had 860 drawers built into the wall structure, plus corresponding components of cupboards and compartments.

Usually the drawers were designed to contain special materials or items of a specific nature. One section of a wall at Hancock had eighty-four numbered drawers of graduated heights, each designed to contain a special species of herb. Similar batteries of drawers occupied entire walls for filing records or materials of the various Shaker shop industries.

Shaker built-ins were usually constructed of pine with each drawer meticulously dovetailed and with tenons going through and pegged into the styles of all door frames. The finished workmanship was either painted in tones of Shaker blue or stained with yellow ocher.

Harmonious appearance of Shaker built-in drawers and cupboards is exemplified by this section of wall which was built in an Enfield, New Hampshire, dwelling early in the nineteenth century. *Photo Courtesy the Henry Francis du Pont Winterthur Museum, Winterthur, Del.*

Built-in storage walls in the Church Family dwelling at Enfield, New Hampshire, contained 860 drawers plus adjoining cupboards. *Photo courtesy the Henry Francis du Pont Winterthur Museum, Winterthur, Del.*

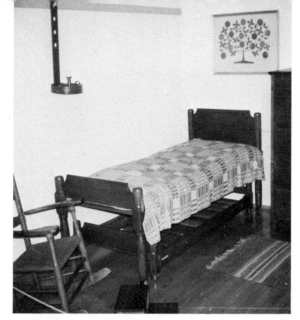

Cherry bed, with trundle bed below, was built at Union Village, Ohio, circa 1830. *Photographed by author at the Warren County Historical Museum, Lebanon, O.*

Shaker Beds

Of all the furniture they produced, the Shakers seem to have paid least attention to the design detailing of their beds. In their utter plainness and simplicity, the designs expressed the Shakers' modesty of purpose more articulately than most of their other furniture. The bed they regarded as a simple platform on which to lie down — and at nightfall, after a hard day's labor, the Shakers required nothing more than a place to rest their weary bodies.

The Shakers called their beds "bed-steads," but nowadays we would call them "cots." For they were so exceptionally short and narrow that one wonders how full-grown adults could fit into them. Usually they were made with plain turned top posts and legs turned on a slight taper. The headboards were straight or slightly curved with corresponding footboards of narrower width. Most frequently the mattress platforms were webbed of rope, which was laced through holes in the side rails and ends. The rope "springs" were covered with slim mattresses filled with cornhusks or feathers.

Almost invariably Shaker beds were fitted with three-inch wooden wheels, notched and pinned crosswise into the bottoms of the legs. These allowed the bed to be drawn out sidewise from

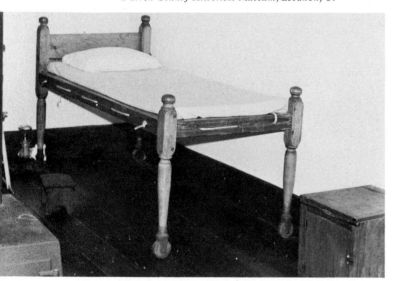

Child's bed made at New Lebanon, New York, circa 1840. *Photographed by author at Hancock Shaker Village, Hancock, Mass.*

Adult cradle made at Harvard, Massachusetts, circa 1840. *Photographed by author at Fruitlands Museums, Harvard, Mass.*

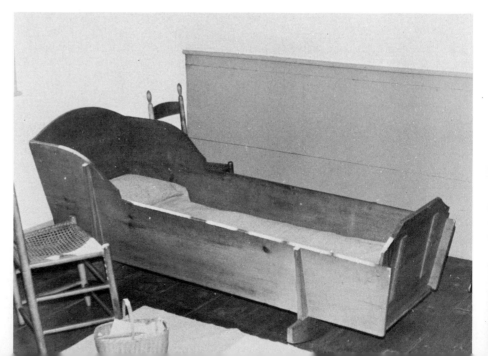

an adjoining wall, but the wheels were not pivoted to provide movement in any other direction.

In the guest rooms reserved for transients, little trundle-bed frames, mounted on similar wheel casters, were tucked under the beds, ready for use by extra guests. Since, at first, the Shakers were accustomed to sleeping on the floor, the little rope-laced trundles were probably regarded as an important contribution to comfort.

It should also be noted that the Shakers of Kentucky designed the first fold-up beds. These folded up flat against the wall. Considering their diminutive dimensions they were probably designed for children.

If the healthy Shakers were not too concerned about the size and comfort of their own beds, they compensated by giving full consideration to the design of beds for the aged and infirm. One design of infirmary bed which was made at Hancock employed wooden cam devices at each end to raise and lower the platform in the manner of hospital beds. Another mercy for the sick and dying was provided with the elongated adult cradles used at the Harvard and Shirley communities. These long, coffinlike cradles were used, apparently, to gently rock the dying Shakers into the rewards of their heavenly rest.

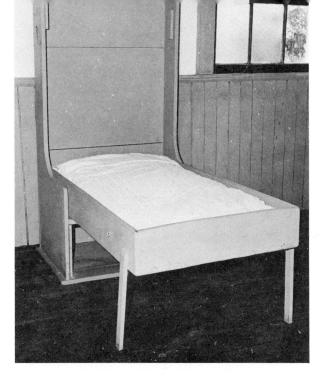

Child's folding bed built by South Union, Kentucky, Shakers, during mid-nineteenth century. *Photographed by Ray Pearson, courtesy the Shaker Museum, Auburn, Ky.*

Infirmary bed, with wooden cam devices for lifting and lowering, was made at New Lebanon, New York, around 1860. *Photo courtesy New York State Museum, Albany, N.Y.*

Trundle bed on wooden rollers went under bedstead in Shakers' guest rooms. *Photographed by author at the Shaker Museum, Old Chatham, N.Y.*

Shaker Service Furniture and Smallcraft

In a strict sense all Shaker furniture belongs in the "service" category. But distinction is made between utilitarian pieces used by the Shakers to facilitate their work as a type apart from the room furniture they designed to bring comfort to their dwellings.

For practically every kind of task they had to perform, the Shakers designed (and quite frequently invented) special furniture, accessories, devices, and tools. In their kitchens they had special cutting tables, chopping blocks, dry sinks, racks, shelves, bins, and benches. Today many of these accessories would be made of metal or plastics. But with their ample supplies of wood — and skill to work it — the Shakers most frequently made their utility pieces of this material.

While the service items were often more heavily constructed than the domestic furniture, they lacked none of the fine Shaker craftsmanship. Drawers were neatly dovetailed, tenons were securely pegged, and all parts were finished with the same care as the chairs, tables, and chests made for the living rooms and dormitories. Ex-

amination of the fascinating old woodbins, reels, looms, drying racks, and "flights of shelves" reveals details of meticulous workmanship which only the Shakers would apply to the making of such things.

As noted elsewhere in this book, the Shakers made their own wooden pails, buckets, churns, and tubs. They also made their own woodenware, including bowls, basins, scoops, ladles, and cutting boards. They designed and made wooden spoons, sieves, rolling pins, mortars and pestles, lanterns, sconces, foot warmers, doughbins, spool racks, canes, crutches, clothes baskets, clothespins, and hundreds of other items — mostly of their own original design.

Shaker utility items are ingeniously styled. Candle scones of western design were made with long stems which were bored with a series of holes to facilitate raising or lowering the candle when the sconce was hung from the ever-present pegboard. Numerous other "hangables" were designed for pegboard mounting, including mirror hangers, pipe boxes, scouring boxes, and various

Butcher block, built at Pleasant Hill, Kentucky, around 1850, was made by mounting a section of sycamore tree trunk on turned maple legs. *Photographed by author at the Shaker Museum, Old Chatham, N.Y.*

Early cobbler's bench, made at New Lebanon, New York, was intricately fitted with drawers and compartments to facilitate work of Shaker shoemakers. *Photo courtesy New York State Museum, Albany, N.Y.*

58

Maple clock reel, commonly made in all Shaker communities, was a flawlessly constructed as a fine piece of furniture. *Photo courtesy the Henry Ford Museum, Dearborn, Mich.*

Shaker "flight of shelves," built at Hancock around 1830, had shelves of graduating widths for storing preserves and dairy products. *Photographed by author at Hancock Shaker Village, Hancock, Mass.*

Shaker sieves and sieve binder were made at New Lebanon, New York. *Photo courtesy New York State Museum, Albany, N.Y.*

Hancock Shaker clothes crate had handles for two Sisters to share load of wet laundry. *Photo courtesy Index of American Design, Washington, D.C.*

Walnut steps, made during mid-nineteenth century at Union Village, Ohio, held metal container for coals — to keep Shaker Sisters' feet warm. *Photographed by author at the Warren County Historical Museum, Lebanon, O.*

Pine set of steps, made at Hancock circa 1830. *Photographed by author at Hancock Shaker Village, Hancock, Mass.*

Neatly dovetailed utility wall box was made during the mid-nineteenth century at Union Village, Ohio. *Photographed by author at the Golden Lamb Inn, Lebanon, O.*

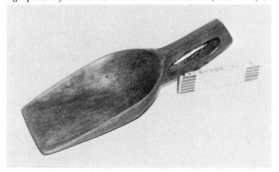

Sugar scoop, circa 1840, was whittled of wood by the Hancock Shakers. *Photographed by author at Hancock Shaker Village, Hancock, Mass.*

Laminated wooden pail, intricately joined of light and dark splines, was made by Ohio Shaker craftsmen. *Photo courtesy Index of American Design, Washington, D.C.*

types of wall containers, which were sometimes delicately fitted with small drawers. The unusually wide assortment of small steps and footstools suggest an aversion on the part of the Believers to keep their feet on the floor.

Shaker Boxes and Oval Carriers

If any one type of Shaker smallcraft could be singled out to demonstrate the perfection of their work, the choice would have to be that of box-making. Delicately constructed and beautifully crafted little boxes were a Shaker specialty. These were made in square, round, and oval shapes.

With their oval boxes, baskets, and carriers, the Shakers created a craft form which was uniquely their own. These distinctively designed containers were made in dozens of different sizes, starting with tiny ovals and graduating up to the handsome full-size boxes and carriers. (They were sold by the dozens in graduated sets.) Some were made as shallow lidded boxes; others as baskets with fixed handles; and still others with lids and fold-down loop handles.

The art of making round and oval carriers originated either at New Lebanon or Watervliet, New York, near the end of the eighteenth century. They were made at all Shaker communities. Construction of their famous carriers was one of the first, and unquestionably the last, of the Shaker craft industries. The last of the Shaker craftsmen, Brother Delmer C. Wilson of the Sabbathday Lake, Maine, community, made his final sets of carriers in 1955.

Despite their appearance of flawless simplicity, construction of the carriers required special skills. They were made of maple, birch, oak, and cherry. The thin side walls were fashioned with delicately shaped fingers which were neatly overlapped and riveted at the connection. Steam bending over a form provided the proper shape. After the shape was secured, the overlapping end fingers were glued and riveted. The bottom, made of thicker wood, was then inserted and tacked around the edges. Early carriers were usually painted. But those made later, particularly during this century, were stained in natural wood tones, then varnished and polished.

Scouring box, made by Union Village, Ohio, Shakers, was used to hold and polish cutlery. *Photographed by author at the Golden Lamb Inn, Lebanon, O.*

Inner walls of dovetailed sewing box are decoratively lined. Ornamental details indicate box was made late in nineteenth century. *Photo courtesy the Henry Ford Museum, Dearborn, Mich.*

Shakers' round and oval boxes and carriers came in graduated sizes of assorted types. *Photo courtesy New York State Museum, Albany, N.Y.*

Shaker oval carriers and boxes retained same designs for over a hundred years. This one is believed to have been built in the 1930's by Brother Delmer Wilson. *Photographed by author at the Shaker Museum, Old Chatham, N.Y.*

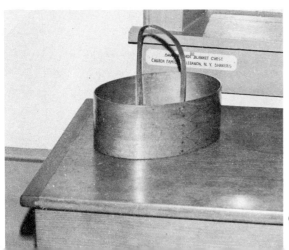

Flawless craftsmanship of Shaker oval boxes is evident in this model made of birch and pine. *Photo courtesy the Henry Ford Museum, Dearborn, Mich.*

This round box, from Canterbury, New Hampshire, was made approximately a hundred years before the one at the left. *Photo courtesy the Henry Ford Museum, Dearborn, Mich.*

This beautifully detailed maple carrier has top inlaid with walnut, oak, and cherry. *Photo courtesy the Henry Ford Museum, Dearborn Mich.*

Decorative bows and upholstered inner lining indicate this oval sewing carrier was the prized possession of a Shaker Sister. It was made at Sabbathday Lake, Maine, early in the twentieth century. *Photo courtesy the Henry Ford Museum, Dearborn, Mich.*

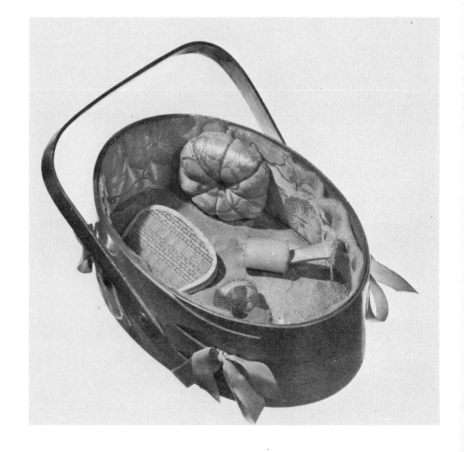

CHAPTER III

SHAKER FURNITURE CONSTRUCTION

Shaker carpentry shop, reconstructed at the Shaker Museum, Old Chatham, New York, contains many of the old tools, machines, and furnishings used by Shaker craftsmen at New Lebanon and other communities. This authentically restored workshop is typical of the spacious and well-equipped rooms in which Shaker craftsmen constructed their furniture. *Photograph by Lees Studio, courtesy the Shaker Museum, Old Chatham, N.Y.*

Shaker Furniture Construction

Construction of Shaker furniture followed few of the conventions established by joiners and cabinetmakers outside the Shaker communities. Of course, the same fundamental practices were applied to the treatment and processing of wood. But the Shakers' individuality and disdain of "worldly superfluity" produced new techniques which made their furniture lighter, stronger, and more practical than that constructed by other craftsmen.

Religious edicts pertaining to furniture construction were just as firmly inscribed as all other rules governing the Shakers' way of work and worship. Their Millennial Laws strictly advocated that the products of their shops must be made "unworldly" by the avoidance of superfluous ornamentation.

"Fancy articles of any kind...superfluously finished, trimmed or ornamented are not suitable for Believers," said the Laws of the Millennium, which were followed by all Shakers. They went on to admonish: "Whatever is fashioned, let it be plain and simple, unembellished by superfluities which add nothing to its goodness and durability. Think not ye can keep the laws of Zion while blending with the forms and fashions of the children of the unclean."

To implement the laws, the Shakers even devised some of their own methods for cutting and joining wood. They were not satisfied with conventional cabinetmaking practices. Instead they modified the basic wood joints, shaping them in their own particular fashion and often introducing entirely new methods. Thus their construction went hand in hand with design to form the uniquely recognizable Shaker style.

Shaker Craftsmen

It is interesting to observe that Shaker craftsmen seldom limited their endeavors to the construction of furniture alone. Indeed, the versatility of many of them — particularly the Elders — went on to include proficiency in performance of many other trades and professions. It was common for a Shaker craftsman to work for a while at furniture construction and then switch to another activity which he was able to do with the same degree of skill.

It has been noted that Isaac Youngs, of New Lebanon, was not only a highly skilled cabinetmaker but was equally competent as a clockmaker, blacksmith, mason, tailor, farmer, teacher, author, and musician. Richard McNemar, leader of the western Shakers, was a classical scholar, poet, author, printer, and editor. But he was also a clever craftsman who applied his skill as a chairmaker, bookbinder, cabinetmaker, and builder of weaving and spinning equipment. Micajah Burnett, who was responsible for the lovely "Georgian-Shaker" architecture at Pleasant Hill, Kentucky, was a highly skilled craftsman as well as being a talented architect and civil engineer. With his own hands he built the superb spiral staircases which grace the Pleasant Hill Trustees' Building.

An almost endless list of versatile Shakers would include Brother Giles Avery, who, as well as being a carpenter and cabinetmaker, was also a stone mason, plasterer, and plumber. Elder Hervey L. Eads of South Union, Kentucky, could turn from woodworking to shoemaking and seed culture. He also worked as a bookbinder, tailor, printer, spinner, metal worker, dentist, author, and eminent bishop-administrator of the Society.

Many of these versatile craftsmen had served their apprenticeship as children in the Shaker communities. They were taught the "arts and mysteries" of various vocations under the tutelage of master craftsmen. When they arrived at an age to select trades they wished to pursue, they were often so multi-skilled that they chose a variety of occupations.

The Shaker covenants and laws stressed the necessity of performing all communal work anonymously. While the rule was sometimes broken, individual craftsmen were not supposed to mark their work with signatures and dates. Such identification was regarded as a display of personal vanity — which, according to the Shakers, detracted from the value of pure workmanship. It is known, however, that some individual Shaker craftsmen excelled in the design and construction of certain types of furniture. These were the especially gifted artisans who created uniquely effective designs and constructional techniques, which were promptly passed along to other craftsmen in other Shaker communities.

Shaker Workshops

With their penchant for neatness and orderliness the Shakers designed their shops just as carefully as their living quarters. Shaker workrooms were models of efficient organization, with everything scientifically planned to facilitate whatever work they had to perform. Usually the carpenters' and joiners' shops — where they made their furniture — were housed in separate buildings, where ample attention was given to the essential aspects of lighting, heating, and ventilation. The woodworking shop was a cheerful place — clean, light, and airy. It was a place where the craftsman could enjoy his occupation.

Tools most frequently used were hung on the walls within easy reach of the busy artisan. Cabinets and workbenches contained dozens of drawers for keeping separate categories of tools, materials, and supplies. Lumber racks and woodworking machinery were located in the most accessible places.

In the design and construction of their shop fur-

nishings the Shakers were no less painstaking than they were in the manufacture of their domestic furniture. Shaker workbenches were, of themselves, things of massive beauty — so much so that a handsome woodworking bench, believed to have been built by the Shakers at Enfield, Connecticut, around 1840, has been effectively installed as an impressive focal feature in the foyer of the art galleries at Fruitlands Museum. Details of this beautifully built bench, as pictured here, show the flawless workmanship which the Shakers applied to construction of all their shop furniture.

Shaker workbenches were as solid as the Rock of Gibraltar. The hardwood tops were of joined planking usually about four inches thick. Hardwood vises, with dovetailed face plates, were fitted to the fronts and ends. Mortised slots were bored at marginal intervals to hold removable bench stops. These were used to hold boards flat for surface planing.

Recessed below the top were rows of drawers. Fronts and backs of each drawer were cleverly dovetailed. Some were fitted with hinged lids to provide another working surface when the drawer was pulled out.

Most Shaker workbenches were constructed of a variety of woods. Frequently white oak or rock maple was used for the tops, while drawer sides, panels, and other parts which were not exposed to wear were made of butternut or pine.

In many Shaker workshops the walls behind the workbenches were occupied by tool cupboards. These, too, were meticulously made. Usually they were fitted with pegs, brackets, and shelves for holding the various tools. When the day's work was done the doors could be closed, with everything neatly secured in its proper place.

It is obvious that the Shakers were just as fastidious about cleanliness in their workshops as they were in the rooms in which they lived. The many drawers and cupboards provided not only a proper place for everything but, when closed, presented smooth surfaces which were easily dusted and kept clean. It is probable that with the completion of each day's work, and undoubtedly betweentimes, Shaker craftsmen put time aside to dust off their benches and equipment and to sweep the floor in preparation for a fresh start.

This beautifully crafted Shaker workbench was so handsomely constructed that it now serves as a massive console beneath the huge "Ruins of Paestum" oil painting, by John Ritto Penniman, which hangs in the art gallery foyer of Fruitlands Museums at Harvard, Massachusetts. The workbench was built by Shaker craftsmen at Enfield, Connecticut, around 1840 — only a few decades after Penniman (1783-1830) painted his impressive "Ruins." *Photographed by author at Fruitlands Museums, Harvard, Mass.*

Details of the Enfield Shaker workbench show the intricately dovetailed end vise with bench stop inserted to hold surface work. Photo at right shows large front vise and space mortising of the top for adjustments of bench stops. Top was joined of heavy white oak planks. Other parts were made of maple, butternut, and pine. Drawer details are shown on the next page. *Photographed by author at Fruitlands Museums, Harvard, Mass.*

Lidded top drawer of the Shaker workbench at Fruitlands Museums provided an additional surface for laying out work. The lid also protected tools and materials from sawdust and shavings which would otherwise drop through the holes mortised along the top. Dovetailed drawers and other details of construction were as meticulously crafted as the finest domestic cabinets. *Photographed by author at Fruitlands Museums, Harvard, Mass.*

This sturdy cabinetmaker's workbench, which extends along an entire section of wall, is believed to have been built for the Church Family's shops at New Lebanon, New York. Some of the early tools were used by Elder George Wickersham, who designed and superintended construction of the main brick building at New Lebanon. *Photographed by author at the Shaker Museum, Old Chatham, N.Y.*

Working Procedure

Shaker craftsmen started their day's work as early as five o'clock in the morning during the summer months and usually a little later (for lack of daylight) during the winter. Undoubtedly, they pondered their constructional problems during the evening hours, or discussed particular problems with their fellow craftsmen. Thus, with their next moves resolved, they were eager to get back to their workbenches at the light of dawn.

Before breakfast, the craftsmen kindled fires in their shop stoves and laid out their materials for the day's work. Almost every day the work varied. One craftsman might be engaged at building a chest of drawers. But he could be called away from this to make something else which was more urgently needed. Sometimes he would spend a day at the sawmill roughing out lumber for future needs. Or he might spend part of his day at the lathe, turning reel spindles, pegs, or chair legs. With these chores performed, he would return to the construction of his chest of drawers.

It is probable that some craftsmen, or apprentices, would devote full time to turning operations or to the processing of parts needed by others. Mortising, dovetailing, and other joinery operations could be performed on a production basis to furnish all craftsmen with supplies of pre-processed parts.

Of course, during the early years, each Shaker craftsman made every part of his projects, from start to finish. And he took pride in the fact that everything was constructed with his own two hands. But as the demand for Shaker furniture increased, it was necessary to employ production procedures in the making of parts and final assembly of finished pieces. However, at no time were the Shakers under compulsion to perform their works as cogs in a factory. They labored at a leisurely pace and were not oppressed with time schedules and progress reports. Whether they built their furniture as individual craftsmen or produced pieces in cooperation with others, all work, regardless of time involved, was performed in the same spirit of patient perfection.

Early auger bit

Shaker Woodworking Tools

The Shakers did not advocate drudgery. Nor did they believe in labor for labor's sake, unassisted by tools and machines which would reduce manual processing. Hence they were constantly seeking new and better tools, devices, machines, and methods to facilitate their work.

Hand tools used by the Shakers were of the finest quality obtainable. While they invented and made many of their own, they were not reluctant to buy the improved tools made outside their communities. They did, in fact, import many of their finest tools from abroad. Thus when searching for tools which are "strictly Shaker" it is almost impossible to separate them from their counterparts used by other carpenters and cabinetmakers during the nineteenth century.

Many of the Shakers' hand tools are now as obsolete as the archaic names they bear. Hardware dealers today would be nonplused if asked to fill orders for froes, holzeaxts beetles, crozes, wimbles, twibils, scorpers, draw knives, or rivers. But these were important hand tools used by the Shakers and other early American craftsmen.

The *froe,* for example, was a heavy blade sharpened along the lower edge and secured, like an ax, to a short handle. The top edge was pounded with a mallet to split rough staves from log sections. The *twibil* was shaped like a pickaxe with a horizontal adze blade at one end and a narrow hatchet

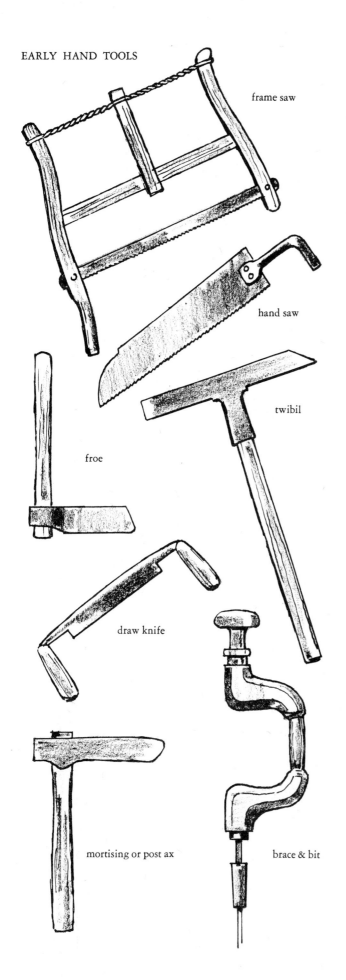

frame saw

hand saw

twibil

froe

draw knife

mortising or post ax

brace & bit

Shaker hand tools include mallets, T reamer, T auger bit, frame saws, and jointer planes. Assorted wooden molding planes are shown on the middle and bottom shelves. Tool chest on floor was Shaker-made around 1840. *Photographed by author at Hancock Shaker Village, Hancock, Mass.*

at the other. It was a general cutting tool used mostly for making rough mortises.

Shaker saws, like those of other early American craftsmen, also came in various types and sizes. The earliest models of crosscut and rip saws were often made with metal handles and oddly shaped blades. Two-man *long saws,* with handles at each end, were used for cutting timber. *Frame saws,* their narrow blades held taut under tension of a twisted leather thong, were used both for straight sawing and for cutting curved shapes. The slim blades prevented binding and allowed free turning.

All Shaker woodworking shops were equipped with an abundance of planes. They varied from the long wooden types used for joining the edges of boards to an infinite assortment of molding planes with cutters ground for rabbeting, grooving, routing, rounding, and forming a variety of other edge shapes.

Early tools used by the Shakers to bore holes were crude and primitive when compared to those we know today. Spiral auger bits with T handles were used for boring large holes, while braces, which seemed too narrow to provide proper leverage, were used to turn the smaller bits.

Shaker planer was built at New Lebanon, New York, around 1860. Note intricate system of pulleys and belts which conveyed power to machines from an overhead shaft. Power was fed into the workshops from water turbines located on nearby streams. Old grindstone, shown at right, and other machines were powered from same source. Later, steam power was also used. *Photographed by author at the Shaker Museum, Old Chatham, N.Y.*

Woodworking Machines

As well as seeking better hand tools, Shaker craftsmen constantly applied their inventive acumen to the development of labor-saving woodworking machines. It has already been noted that Sister Tabitha Babbitt, of the Harvard Shakers, invented the power circular saw blade in 1810. This invention virtually revolutionized the production of lumber. For as well as eliminating the strenuous manual labor involved in hand-sawing planks from logs,

it also vastly improved the production of timbers, planks, boards, and wooden parts used in construction.

Applying the circular-saw principle of revolving power, in 1828 Brothers Amos Bisby and Henry Bennett of the New Lebanon Shakers invented a tongue-and-groove machine. This not only accelerated the processing of lumber but also introduced the strong tongue-and-groove joinery which the

Shaker ingenuity was evident in their conversion of a treadle sewing machine to perform the functions of jig saw. They replaced the needle with a thin sawblade which cut wood with the same up-and-down motions. *Photographed by author at the Shaker Museum, Old Chatham, N.Y.*

An earlier model of treadle jig saw, used by the Shakers of New Lebanon, is believed to have been purchased from an outside source in Kentucky. *Photograph by Lees Studio, courtesy the Shaker Museum, Old Chatham, N.Y.*

Shakers applied to the boarding of floors, table tops, and other broad wooden surfaces.

Throughout the nineteenth century and well into the twentieth the Shakers were constantly developing new ideas for the design of machines to expedite their work and eliminate manual labor. As well as applying their own ideas they were always on the lookout for new machines and devices made outside their communities. Thus their woodworking shops were equipped with efficient circular saws, planers and joinery machines, scroll saws, lathes, mortisers, sanders, shapers, and various other machines.

Many of the early lathes, mortisers, scroll saws, and other woodworking machines were manually operated. Some were ingeniously designed. One model of scroll saw, devised during later years for the shop at New Lebanon, was mounted on a sewing-machine stand. The treadle action of the flywheel provided up and down motion of a cutting blade which was rigged to replace the sewing-machine needle.

Another treadle-action jigsaw was ingeniously equipped with bellows, attached to a tube which led to the sawing surface. The treadle motion activated the bellows, as well as the cutting blade, to force a stream of air through the tube, blowing away the sawdust and thus making it easier for the craftsman to follow the cutting line.

Early wood-turning lathes were also treadle-powered, with heavy flywheels mounted above the shafts to maintain inertial momentum and keep the work revolving at a steady rate. Later, of course, the lathes were connected with pulleys and belts to overhead power shafts. But the foot lathes continued to be used for turning wooden bowls, pegs, and other small items.

Most of the machines were powered by water turbines. At New Lebanon a complex of dams was built along an adjoining mountainside to provide a steady flow of water to turn the waterwheels. Power was conveyed to the workshops with a series of pulleys and belts. In the shops, overhead shafts transmitted the power to individual machines.

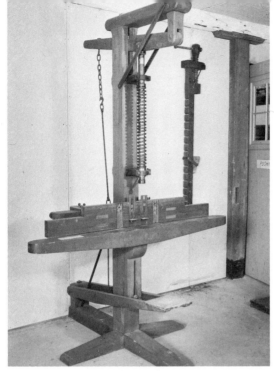

This formidable mortising machine is believed to have been designed and built by the Shakers of Watervliet, New York, around 1860. *Photograph by Lees Studio, courtesy the Shaker Museum, Old Chatham, N.Y.*

Early mortising machine, operated with a hand lever, was used by Shaker craftsmen at New Lebanon, New York, around 1840. *Photographed by author at the Shaker Museum, Old Chatham, N.Y.*

The original tongue-and-groove machine was invented by Henry Bennett and Amos Bisby of the New Lebanon, New York, Shakers in 1828. The water-powered mechanism accelerated production of tongue-and-grooved boards used in Shaker construction. *Photograph by Lees Studio, courtesy the Shaker Museum, Old Chatham, N.Y.*

Treadle lathe, used as early as 1840 by wood turners at New Lebanon, New York, was operated by foot power. Momentum of heavy flywheel kept work revolving smoothly. *Photographed by author at the Shaker Museum, Old Chatham, N.Y.*

This heavy-duty water-powered lathe was used to turn everything from chair legs to small bowls. It was first used at the New Lebanon workshops around 1870 and continued to function until the community closed. The turned shafts shown at left are Shaker chair legs. Old tools, hanging on wall, are of mixed periods. The wood-turning tools, shown here, were imported by the Shakers from England. They are made of the finest steel by Butcher of Sheffield. *Photograph by Lees Studio, courtesy the Shaker Museum, Old Chatham, N.Y.*

Lumber and Materials

With wide tracts of woodland adjoining the sites of most of their communities, the Shakers did not want for materials with which to construct their buildings and furniture. Most common among the woods they used was clear white pine. During the early years of settlement, pine grew in abundance throughout eastern New York and New England. Moreover, the virgin pine trees (sometimes called "pumpkin pine") grew to great girth and could be sawed to produce planks more than three feet wide. Because of its straight growth much of this pine was used for the tall masts and booms of merchant marine and navy sailing ships of the United States and countries abroad. Hence the noble pumpkin pines of early America, which the Shakers used for their furniture, were vastly overharvested, and as a special species, the great trees are now almost extinct.

The Shakers used pine for making table tops and other wide surfaces. Often one broad board sufficed for the entire surface. Pine was also used for cupboards, chests, desks, benches, counters, boxes, washstands, and other articles. For as well as eliminating the additional work of joining boards together to form broad surfaces, pine was the easiest of woods to work — and it was well adapted to the simple shapes of Shaker designs.

For the parts of their furniture exposed to tougher wear, or when extra structural strength was required, the Shakers used hardwoods. Hardwoods were also the usual choice for parts turned on the lathe. Maple, birch, cherry, and walnut were selected for fashioning table legs and stretchers, pedestal stands, chair and bed posts, and other structural parts.

Sometimes an entire piece of furniture was made of one type of wood. But the Shakers were not reluctant to mix their woods — particularly if one wood was better adapted than another for making certain parts. Thus their tables were made with hardwood bases and softwood tops; their chairs might have rungs of ash, oak, or hickory while the posts are maple or birch.

In western workshops, basswood, beech, and butternut were often used in place of pine. White oak, chestnut, elm, hemlock, and spruce were often mixed to form one piece of furniture. Some articles of Shaker wooden ware, such as bowls, scoops, and ladles, were often fashioned of fruitwood. A sturdy butcher block built at Pleasant Hill, Kentucky (see page 116), was made of a massive section of sycamore tree trunk.

About the only decoration the Shakers would tolerate was that inherent in beautiful wood graining. They referred to the better grades of lumber as "clear-stuf" — and craftsmen were constantly alert to select boards of superior grain patterns to enrich the surfaces of their finer pieces. They seemed to have particular admiration for the grain patterns of birds-eye and curly maple and used these woods extensively to turn the legs of chairs and tables.

Unlike other craftsmen outside their communities, the Shakers regarded all veneers as deceitful; as a "worldly hoax" intended to disguise inferior woods and workmanship. They also had little respect for the elegance of mahogany — although they did use it frugally in their limited production of later years.

Manufacture of Lumber

Sawmills came first among the project priorities of most Shaker settlements. Intricate systems of dams, waterwheels, and turbines conveyed power from nearby streams to the sawing machinery inside the mills. Here the logs, taken from adjoining forests, were ripped into planks and boards.

With characteristic patience the Shaker craftsmen carefully stacked their planks for extended periods of outdoor seasoning. Then, with special drying kilns of their own invention, they slowly cured the wood to eliminate any future risks of warping or splitting. It was then ready to be examined and graded and brought into the workshop for dressing down to required widths and thicknesses.

It should be noted that the Shakers' extreme care in the curing of their lumber contributed significantly to the endurance of their furniture. Many of the tops of tables at Shaker museums are just as straight and perfectly flat today as they were when they left the joiners' workshops well over a century ago.

This fine old Hancock rocker is colorfully "upholstered" in checkerboard patterns of worsted tape. Tasteful combinations of weaving patterns and colors complemented the natural wood or lustrous ebony finishes of the rocker frames. At one time the Shakers produced as many as fifty combinations of colors and woven patterns. *Photographed by author at Hancock Shaker Village, Hancock, Mass.*

Weaving Materials

Seats of chairs and rockers built by the Shakers before 1830 were commonly covered with woven "splint" or "rush." Splint was made of thin, pliable strips of hardwood — usually hickory, ash, or maple. Rush was produced as a cord of twisted straw. Leather and cane were also used.

Sometime after 1830, the Shakers introduced colorful worsted tapes — which they called "listing." These were woven by the Shaker Sisters, on special looms, in a variety of colors and patterns. The many color combinations and assorted woven designs of Shaker tapes brought bright new accents to the already attractive chairs and rockers.

Some excellent weaving tapes, duplicating colors and patterns of those used by the Shakers, may still be obtained from Mrs. James S. Brown, P.O. Box 174, Lee, Massachusetts 01238. Rush, splint, and caning materials are obtainable from the H. H. Perkins Co., 228 Shelton Avenue, New Haven, Connecticut.

The earliest Shaker chairs and rockers were "bottomed" with hardwood splint. Narrow, pliable strips of ash, hickory, maple, and other bendable woods were specially selected and treated to prevent splitting. *Photographed by author at the Shaker Museum, Old Chatham, N.Y.*

Rush

Colored tape — checkerboard pattern

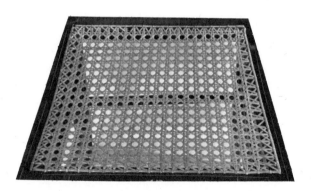

Fine cane

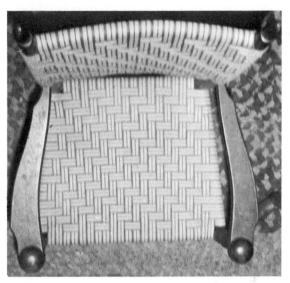

Striped tape — herringbone step pattern

Broad cane

Striped tape — basketweave

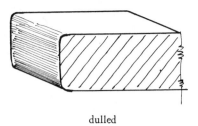

dulled

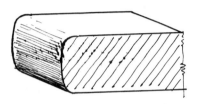

slightly rounded

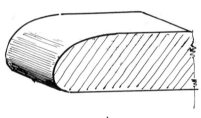

roundnose

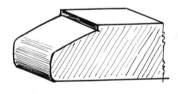

thumbnose — beveled

thumbnose — rounded

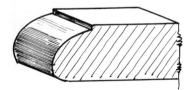

Shaker Shapes

The practical plainness of Shaker furniture was produced with simple shapes. Unlike early American craftsmen working outside their communities, the Shakers did not go in for elaborate scrollwork, ornamental turning, or any other extravagance of curved shaping which did not contribute to the essential functions of their workmanship.

Edges of table tops, dressers, chests, and stands were often simply dulled to remove sharpness — with no pretense of special shaping. Sometimes the edges were slightly rounded or softened to form a rounded nose. But this was probably done as a concession to ease of handling rather than appearance. Later, however, the distinctive "thumb-nose," shouldered-edge shapes, shown at left, appeared along the tops of chests of drawers and other articles. However, even this slight modification was rarely applied to the larger service pieces.

Since the Shakers disdained the "worldly show" of ornamental brasses and decorative hardware of any sort, they invariably made their drawer pulls, knobs, handles, and pegs of plainly turned wood. The assortment of such items, photographed at the right, shows the simple shapes of turning which were followed in communities of both the East and West. As illustrated, the pegs were sometimes delicately threaded to screw securely into holes of the joining boards.

Almost invariably, Shaker shapes were governed by the necessity of function. Even the handsome wooden buckets, with their graceful handles and softly lapped hoops, were shaped that way to provide greater strength and endurance. About the only deliberate beautification of parts came later, when chairs and rockers were constructed with delicately tapered back posts often terminating at the tops with dainty, pointed finials. But the finials were also ovoid and ball-shaped, suggesting the Shaker craftsman only intended to provide handy back grips for lifting the chairs.

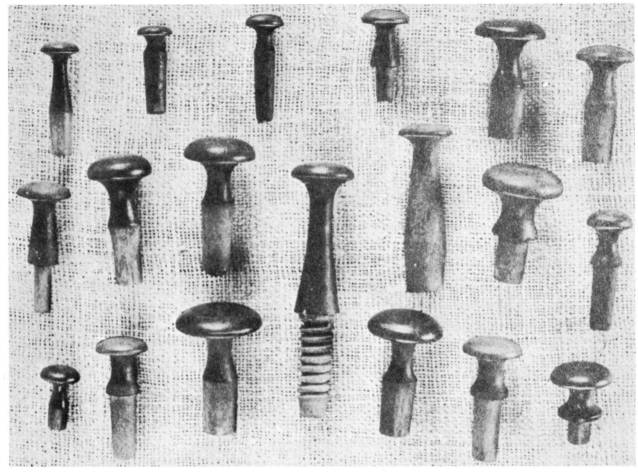

Pegs and pulls, turned on Shaker Lathes, graduated from tiny drawer pulls, no more than half an inch long, to the larger threaded pegs which were fastened to narrow boards to make the pegboards found in all Shaker dwellings. As may be noted, drawer pulls, large or small, were of the same general shape. They were turned of maple, cherry, and other hardwoods. *Photo from the book "Shaker Furniture," courtesy Mrs. Edward Deming Andrews.*

The old oaken bucket, as the Shakers designed it, was probably made of maple and hickory. Note graceful shape of the pegged handle and overlapping hoop. *Photo courtesy the New York State Museum, Albany, N.Y.*

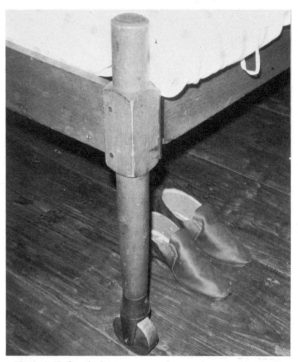

Scrolled leaf support of an early Hancock stretcher table was pivoted on hardwood pins which pierced the dadoed top and bottom fittings. *Photographed by author at Hancock Shaker Village, Hancock, Mass.*

Typical Shaker bed post was stub-turned at the top and tapered at the bottom. Rails were mortised and pegged into square section. Note wooden rollers for moving bed away from wall. Shaker shoes, below bed, are not too unlike "mod" footgear of today. *Photographed by author at Fruitlands Museums, Harvard, Mass.*

Shaker shapes, as applied to details of their chairs and rockers, include, from left to right: (1) slightly scrolled rocker arm with "mushroom" tenon cap; (2) delicately pointed finial of tapered back post; (3) ball finial of western chair; and (4) slash-bent back post of common utility chairs. *Photographed by author at eastern and western Shaker museums.*

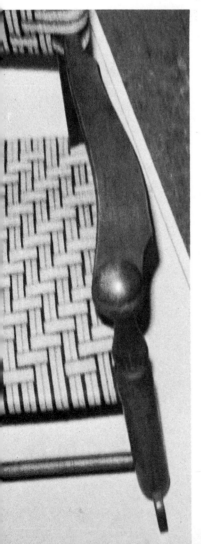

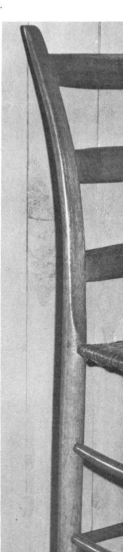

Joinery

Shaker furniture derived its strength and endurance from the clever joinery methods the craftsmen employed to put the parts together. The nails and screws they first used were crudely made. Early nails were hand-wrought, like those sketched below, and early wood screws were blunt-ended, with irregular threads and off-center slots. Later, both types of fasteners were precision-made on machines.

Adhesives used by the Shakers were especially effective. Many of the old table tops and surface panels, edge-bonded of boards put together over a century ago, are as solid today as they were when originally glued. The "animal glues" used by the Shakers were obtained from the hoofs of horses and other animals. The melted concoction was poured into shallow pans and cooled to form glass-like sheets. The sheets were then broken into flakes and boiled to make each fresh batch of glue. (Boiling in skimmed milk was supposed to make the glue water-resistant.) This was applied hot to the joining parts, which were then clamped together until the glue dried.

Edge Joints

Obviously, with their early invention of the tongue-and-groove machine, the Shakers usually joined their boards togethed by the tongue-and-groove method. Such edge joints, secured with glue, assured a lasting bond. They were sometimes varied with double grooves and splines. Some surfaces, however, were made up of boards simply butt-

EARLY WOOD SCREWS AND NAILS

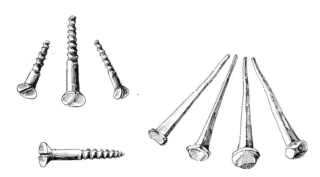

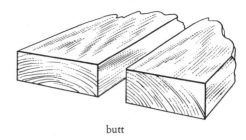

butt

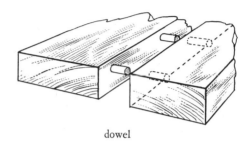

dowel

tongue-and-groove

rabbet

spline

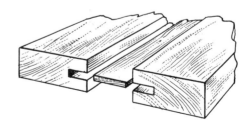

81

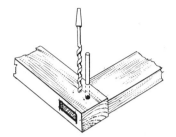

through tenon, pegged

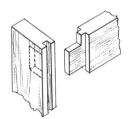

haunched and grooved

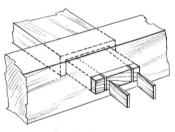

wedged

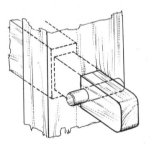

keyed — horizontal

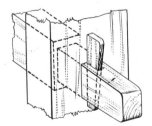

keyed — vertical

joined and glued along the edges. The endurance of these pieces again attests to the strength of Shaker glues. Other edge joints were rabbeted together, thus providing additional edges for application of adhesives.

While it would require some special type of X-ray equipment to determine whether the boards of some existing Shaker pieces were simply butted together or reinforced with dowels, it is probable that dowels were also used.

Mortise and Tenon Joints

Working in their own independent way, Shaker craftsmen made their mortise-and-tenon joints differently from their contemporaries. On all their framed pieces they ran the mortises and tenons clear through the connecting parts. Then, to be sure the joints would never come apart, they reinforced the assembly with glue and hardwood pegs. On heavier pieces they split the tenons, where they came through the connecting mortises, and inserted wedges to spread them for tighter fit. A variation of such fitting called for the cutting of long tenons which protruded beyond the connecting mortises. The protruding tenons were bored to receive tapered "keys," which were inserted in vertical or horizontal positions. As the keys were pounded into place they drew the tenon shoulders snugly flush against the mortised member.

Lapped Joints

Many pieces of Shaker furniture were constructed with parts overlapped and joined to form flush assemblies. Such joints included the reciprocating end-lap, middle-lap and cross-lap types most frequently used for frame construction, and for forming the bases of utility stands, clock reels, and other items. Lapped joints were usually reinforced with nails, screws, and glue.

Sometimes, when extra strength was required, the patient Shaker craftsmen would cut the overlapping end connections in dovetail shapes. An ingenious half-dovetailed lap joint, which appears to be uniquely Shaker, was used for bracing the tops and legs of meetinghouse benches. This construction is shown on page 89.

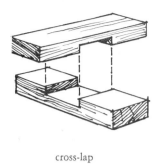

cross-lap

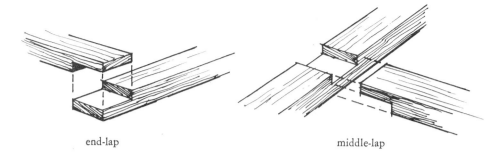

end-lap

middle-lap

LAPPED JOINTS

DOVETAILED MIDDLE-LAP

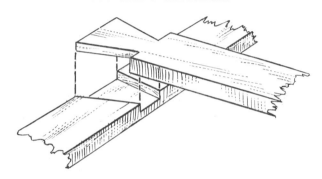

Massive construction of Shaker trestle tables involved lapping of dadoed cross cleat into slot at top of post. This was secured with hardwood dowels. Connection of center rail, shown at bottom, was joined with the same dowels driven (as shown above) from outside the post. All joints were reinforced with glue. *Photographed by author at the Shaker Museum, Old Chatham, N.Y.*

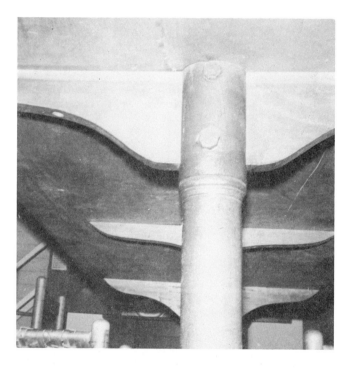

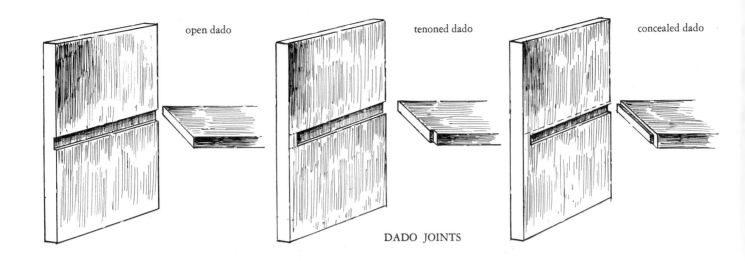

open dado   tenoned dado   concealed dado

DADO JOINTS

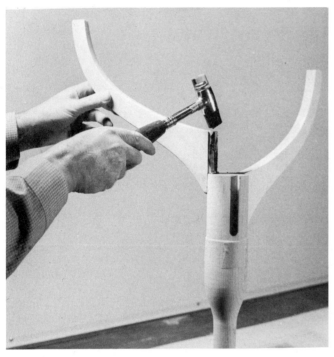

Sliding dovetail stem-leg assembly of Shaker pedestal. (See page 90.) *Photo by author.*

Dado and Dovetail Joints

Dados, which are simple grooves cut *across* a board, were used by the Shakers for shelf construction and for the fitting of case frames.

Dovetail joints, of the types illustrated, are the most conspicuous constructional features of all Shaker furniture. Aside from neatness of appearance, their exceptional strength and durability caused them to be used on almost everything the Shakers built. Because dovetailing is such a singularly important feature of Shaker construction the next six pages are devoted to detailed examination of the various types of dovetail joints.

The step-by-step constructional photos, which follow page 86, are intended to penetrate into the anatomy of Shaker furniture by showing how dovetails were actually cut and fitted and the methods used by Shaker craftsmen to put the parts of their furniture together.

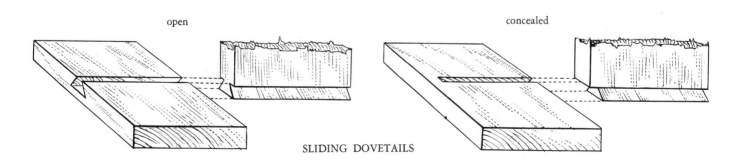

open   concealed

SLIDING DOVETAILS

Bottom structure of Shaker drop-leaf table shows repeated use of dovetails and finger joints. Because of the extra strength and endurance which dovetailed joinery contributed to their work, the Shakers applied this clever construction to almost everything they built. Finger joints, cut on the dovetail principle, made a strong connection for pivoting the gate-leg leaf support. *Photo courtesy Index of American Design, Washington, D.C.*

The scrupulous Shakers insisted that the backs as well as the fronts of drawers must be precisely dovetailed. Other craftsmen were not so particular about hidden details of construction. *Photographed by author at Fruitlands Museums, Harvard, Mass.*

DOVETAIL JOINTS

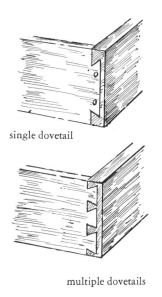

single dovetail

multiple dovetails

open dovetails

dovetail fitting

"feathered" dovetails

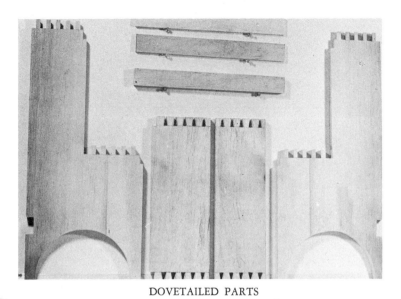

DOVETAILED PARTS

ASSEMBLED STEPS

Dovetailing Steps

(See measured drawing page 108.)
Shaker craftsmen were such master dovetailers that they probably perfected faster and better ways of cutting these joints than the tedious procedures pictured here. However, this is one way of making dovetail joints with hand tools — and, by way of demonstration, it may be illustrative to reconstruct the Shaker set of steps, first made at Hancock, Massachusetts, around 1835. The step-by-step photo sequence shows how the dovetails were cut and fitted together.

Of course, these are only the simple, open dove-tails which the Shakers used for outside corner construction. The more complicated concealed dovetails, which were embedded in the drawer fronts, involving routing out the front board to receive the side dovetails. This they accomplished with routing tools and sharp chisels.

While the Shakers were highly skilled crafts-men — especially adroit in their use of hand tools — during later years they undoubtedly used their routing machines for mass production of dove-tailed parts.

1. Paper template may be used to mark shape of dovetails.

2. Dovetail marking is squared across ends.

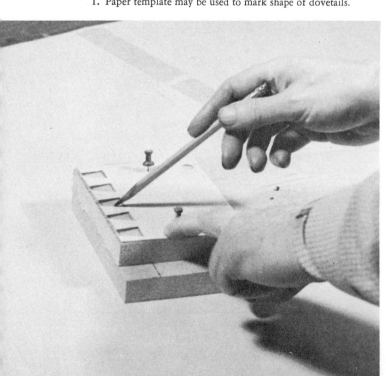

3. Series of saw cuts are made between dovetail markings.

4. Sharp chisel removes sawed space between dovetails.

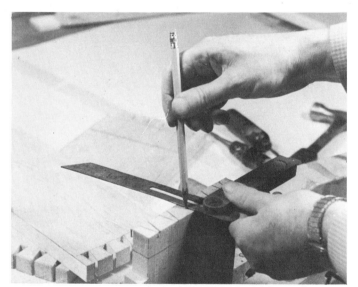

5. Shape of dovetails is scribed on end of joining board.

6. Bevel gauge guides marking of firm lines on joining ends.

7. Joining dovetails are sawed and chiseled as shown in steps 3 and 4, then fitted together.

8. Dovetailed parts are gently pounded together to test final fit.

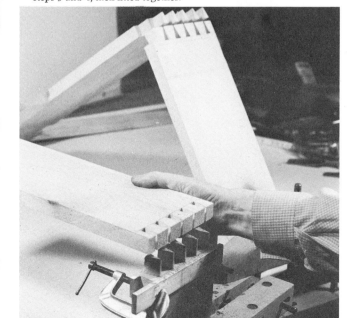

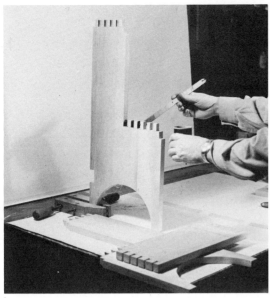

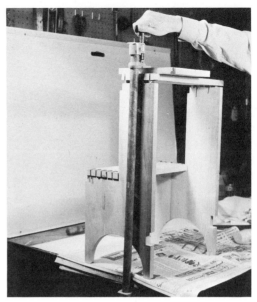

9. Glue is applied to connecting dovetails of both pieces.

10. Connecting dovetails are pressed together under clamp pressure.

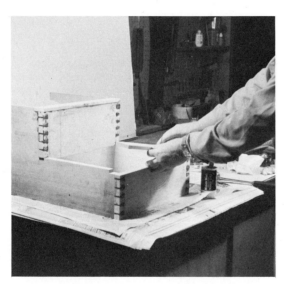

11. Facing strips are glued to rabbets of front edges.

12. After glue has dried, dovetails are planed flush.

13. Edges are dulled with file and sandpaper.

14. Finished dovetails fit flush to sanded surfaces.

All photos by author

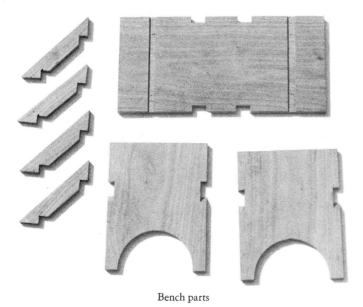

Bench parts

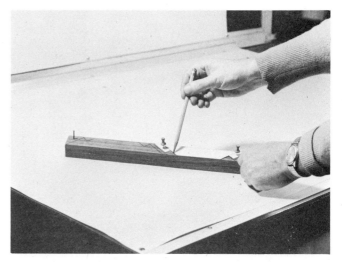

Half-dovetailed bracing strips are marked from paper template.

Dovetailed Bench Bracing

(See measured drawing page 109.)
The classical Shaker meeting-house benches and small benches like the one shown below (which was first made by the Shakers of Hancock around 1830) were strengthened with half-dovetailed bracing strips. These were diagonally dadoed into the edges of the tops and legs. When glued and nailed into the dado cutouts, as shown at right, the half-dovetailed braces provided construction of maximum strength. Because of this construction, Shaker benches could be made of lighter wood and still support heavy loads without bending at the middle.

After mitering and notching the ends, braces are fitted into edge cutouts connecting legs to top.

Single brad and glue secures dovetails in cutouts of top and legs. Protruding ends are planed flush.

Shaker bench with half-dovetailed bracing

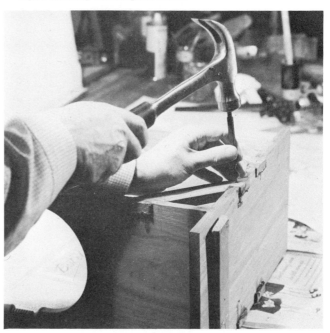

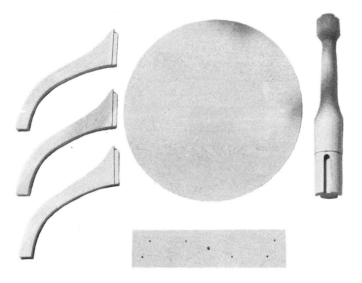

Pedestal parts

Assembled pedestal stand

Assembly of Slot-Dovetailed Pedestal Stand

(See measured drawing page 182.)
The exquisite turning, which distinguished the original Shaker model of this pedestal stand (see page 182) has not been duplicated in this reproduction model. But to show the construction — which is the same — this one was assembled from a modified kit. Thus, while the legs were recut to conform to authentic design, the stem turning lacks the grace of the original.

It will be noted that the slot-dovetailed connections of legs and stem, when reinforced with glue, assures an everlasting bond. For the spread of the dovetailed tenons guarantees the legs will never come loose.

As an extra measure of precaution against splitting, Shaker craftsmen cut the curved legs on the bias of the wood so that the grain followed parallel to the curve.

Dovetailed leg tenons are fitted into stem slots. Spread of the dovetails locks the parts together.

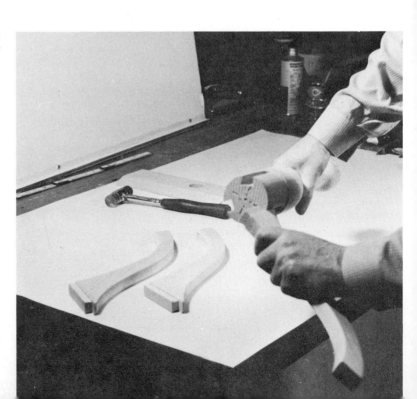

Cross cleat is glued to top tenon of stem.

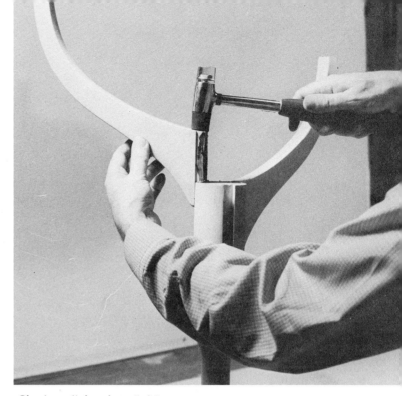

Glue is applied to dovetailed leg tenons and inside the stem slots. Tenon is then gently tapped into slot.

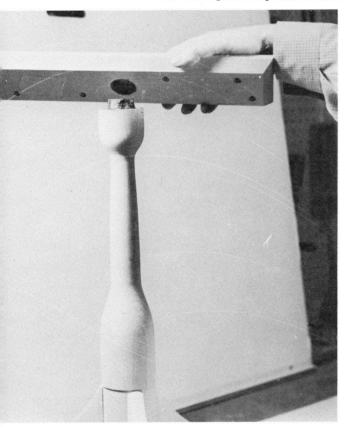

For final assembly, cleat is fastened with screws to undersurface of top.

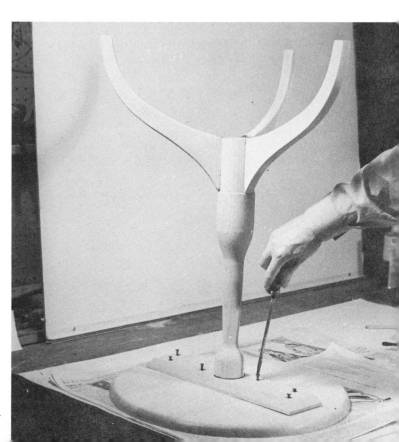

Jigs and accessories used for construction of Shaker boxes and oval carriers include templates for fingered sidewalls, lid and bottom patterns, and clamps (including clothespins) for holding parts together during assembly.

Pictured below are some of the original template molds used for shaping the steam-bent sidewalls. *Top photo taken by author at the Shaker Museum, Old Chatham, N.Y. Bottom photo courtesy the New York State Museum, Albany, N.Y.*

Construction of Oval Boxes and Carriers

(See measured drawing page 112.)

Shaker construction of round and oval boxes and loop-handled wooden baskets — or "carriers," as they called them — started in the eighteenth century and continued until Brother Delmer C. Wilson, of the Sabbathday Lake Shakers, made his final set of carriers during the 1950's.

The devices and tools used for construction of Shaker boxes and carriers, pictured above, included templates of the "fingers" (or "lappers") for making the overlapping sides; solid forms, called "template molds," of the various shapes and sizes; templates of the bottom shapes; and special clamps.

Construction involved shaping of the thin side walls to conform to templates. The sides were steam-bent over the molds. After the shape was secured, the overlapping fingers were glued and riveted. The bottom, made of thicker wood, was then inserted and tacked around the edges.

Early carriers were usually made with maple side walls and pine bottoms. Some, depending on the community of their origin, had walls of birch, oak, or cherry. They were usually painted. But those made during this century were often stained in natural wood tones, then varnished and polished.

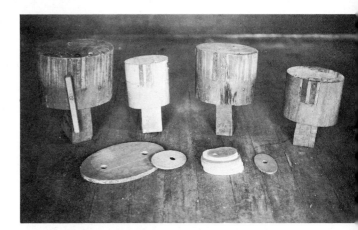

Sets of oval boxes were made by the Shakers in graduated sizes. They were usually sold by the dozen. Assorted types shown on counter were of same construction as the loop-handled carriers. *Photographed by author at the Shaker Museum, Old Chatham, N.Y.*

CHAPTER IV

SHAKER FURNITURE FINISHING

Shaker Furniture Finishing

Shaker varnish finishes involved preliminary application of stains which were rubbed with rags to bring out the natural wood graining. Several coats of spar varnish were then applied. As each coat dried it was rubbed down with pumice-stone powder to produce a lustrous final polish. *Photograph by author.*

The Shakers were just as particular about the finishing of their furniture as they were about the craftsmanship which went into its construction. They went to great lengths to compound proper paints, stains, and varnishes. And despite their precepts of plainness, they were not at all averse to the use of bright and cheerful colors.

As with all things Shaker, however, the leaders of the Society regulated the ingredients of the paints and finishes. Moreover, they selected the colors and prescribed the proper places for their use. Thus, in all communities the interior wood trim of the meeting houses was painted blue. This varied from the pale "robin's egg" used in the communities of Maine to the darker shades used elsewhere. The floors were painted a reddish yellow in the dwellings and a brighter yellow in the shops. Some furniture (especially the "bed-steads") was painted bottle-green. Shop furniture, utility benches, work tables, stools, steps, wood boxes, and other service items were painted in various tones of red.

At first Shaker furniture was simply covered with protective coats of paint, but it was soon observed that when the paint was thinned and applied as a penetrating stain, the natural wood graining which showed through enhanced the appearance of the work. This led to development of oil and water stains. Such stains were covered with varnish, which was polished with pumice stone to produce natural wood finishes.

Recipes of Old Shaker Finishes

In his extensive research, Dr. Andrews came across a Watervliet "common-place book," circa 1849, which contained recipes for making Shaker finishes. Ingredients of some of these, as quoted here, may presently be hard to find:

Red stain for wood, leather, papers
Take 1½ oz. Brazeil dust, put it in 1 pt. of Alcohol — warm it a little in water Bath, or on a Stove — say ½ hour, then put in, say, about One teaspoon full of Bookbinders' Acid, which will turn it a beautiful red . . .

Laker [that is, "lacquer"]
Take 1 Gall. Linseed Oil
1 lb. Literage ["litharge"]
¾ lb. Red Lead, ground fine. Boil slowly until it is so thick, it will not strike through writing paper, which will take the most of a day to accomplish. Stir it often, and add when partly cool One Gall. Spts. Turpentine, and bottle for use.

White with blue shade
To 100 lbs. White Lead or Zinc, add 1 oz. Prusian Blue and 1 oz. Lampblack. Take the Lead and stir in Black and Blue, until you get the shade you desire.

Another early Hancock manuscript, also uncovered by Dr. Andrews, offers these Shaker finishing recipes:

To Color blue on wood
Pulverize 1 oz. best Spanish Float Indigo, put it into 7 ozs. Sulphuric Acid in a glass vessel — let it stand 2 days. When used put a quanity sufficient into pure water and add Pearlast till the shade suits.

To Color Pink or Red on Wood
Put one lb. of chipped Nicaraqa Wood to 1 Gal. pure water, boil 10 minutes in a brass vessel; then brush or dip the article in it and after brush it over with the following mixture, viz. to 1 oz. Muriatic acid add 1 oz. Grained Tin, leave out the stopper of the bottle till the Tin is dissolved. When the wood is dry — varnish.

Varnish, at first, was sparingly used by the Shakers. The Millennial Laws of 1845 decreed: "Varnish if used in dwelling houses, may be applied only to the moveables therein, as the following: viz. Tables, stands, bureaus, cases of drawers, writing desks or boxes, drawer faces, chests, chairs, etc., etc."

Natural Wood Finishes

Toward the middle of the nineteenth century, the Shakers developed their own copal and "jappan" varnishes. They also prepared brown and honey-colored stains which were compounded in oil, water, and spirits in about the same way they are made today. Shellacs and lacquers were also used. And for the treatment of darker hardwoods, such as walnut and cherry, they used linseed oil.

Since the Shakers were always willing to try new and better materials and methods, they would probably admire the improved stains, paints, and clear finishes produced nowadays by modern chemistry. And such polishing conveniences as garnet paper and steel wool would undoubtedly meet with their approval. Beyond these innovations, however, the methods employed for finishing Shaker furniture, as shown in the accompanying step-by-step photo sequences, would probably remain just about the same.

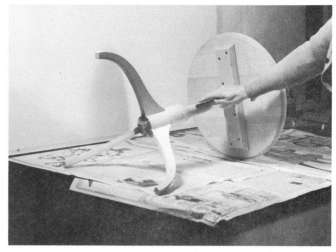

1. Before applying stain, all parts are thoroughly sanded.

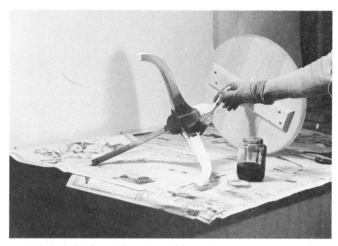

2. Stain is first brushed on legs and stem, then on top.

3. Soft rag is used to remove excess stain and bring out wood graining.

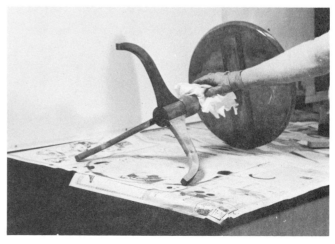

4. After stain dries, first coat of varnish is brushed evenly on all parts.

5. When first coat of varnish is thoroughly dry (24 hours) it is rubbed with fine steel wool.

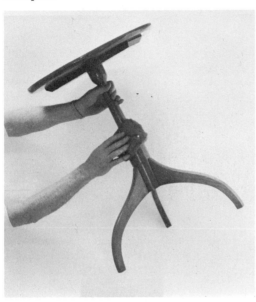

6. Stem and legs are also rubbed with steel wool. Second coat of varnish is then applied.

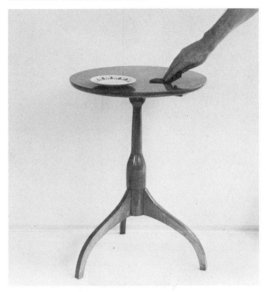

7. After second coat of varnish dries, work is rubbed evenly with fine (wet or dry) garnet paper.

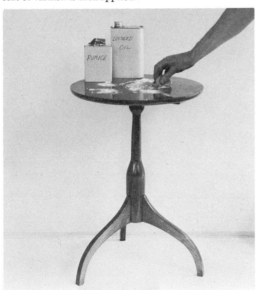

8. Final coat of varnish is polished with fine pumice-stone powder and linseed oil.

9. Lustrous final finish is obtained by waxing and rubbing with soft cloth.

1. Heavy oil stain is brushed over all parts of Shaker steps.

2. Stain is immediately rubbed off to expose wood grain and develop uniform tone.

Simple Shellac Finish

With the ingredients specified in old finishing recipes, Shaker finishes can be exactly duplicated today, and the colors can still be bought at several places specializing in "Shaker paints."

Of course, during later years the Shakers did know about shellac. And because of its ease of application and rapid drying they undoubtedly used it for finishing much of their furniture. Unlike varnish, which requires long periods of drying between coats, shellacs, when properly thinned with alcohol, dries within two hours after application.

Shellac is particularly suitable for finishing pine. Indeed, orange shellac alone — without stain — becomes enhanced with the natural tones and patina of age.

However, if stain is used, heavier mixtures are recommended. This is because the porosity of pine absorbs thin stains unevenly, causing blotchy effects. Heavy stains can be "worked" until the wood grain is evenly exposed.

The accompanying photos show how the Shakers might have applied a simple shellac finish to the pine set of steps they first produced at Hancock, around 1830. (The original Shaker model, however, was probably painted red!)

3. After stain is thoroughly dry, thin coat of shellac is applied.

4. Between coats, shellac is smoothed with fine steel wool.

1. Fine sandpaper is used to smooth all parts of Shaker bench.

2. Boiled linseed oil is brushed on sanded parts. It penetrates to enrich walnut grain.

3. After rubbing off excess oil, second and third coats are applied.

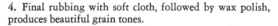

4. Final rubbing with soft cloth, followed by wax polish, produces beautiful grain tones.

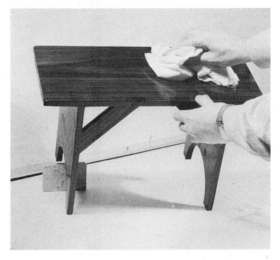

Linseed Oil Finish

The Shakers found many uses for linseed oil. They used it as an ingredient of their paints, stains, and varnishes; as a wood preservative; and by itself as a natural wood finisher. To bring out the natural beauty of dark woods — particularly walnut — nothing surpasses linseed oil. It penetrates into the wood and enriches the graining. Moreover, wood which is treated with oil is amply protected against ordinary damage, and the finish may be renewed at any time with fresh applications.

For finishing Shaker reproductions, such as the copy of the Hancock Shaker bench shown here, *boiled* linseed oil is thinned slightly with turpentine. Two tablespoons of vinegar may be added to each pint of oil. The mixture is then applied as shown in the accompanying photographs. For best results, two or three coats should be brushed on. Between coats, excess oil is rubbed off with a soft rag.

After a drying period of two or three days, the final coat may be polished with wax to produce a soft luster. It will be observed that the oil penetrates into the wood — and once it has hardened it does not soil covers or clothing.

CHAPTER V

SHAKER SMALLCRAFT
with Museum-Measured Drawings

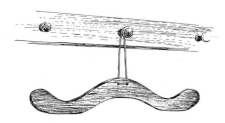

SISTERS' GARMENT HANGER AND PEGBOARD.
Ohio and Kentucky, mid-nineteenth century.

BROTHERS' GARMENT HANGER. Ohio and Kentucky, mid-nineteenth century.

MULTIPLE CLOTHES RACK, New Lebanon, circa 1850. Hancock Shaker Village, Hancock, Mass.

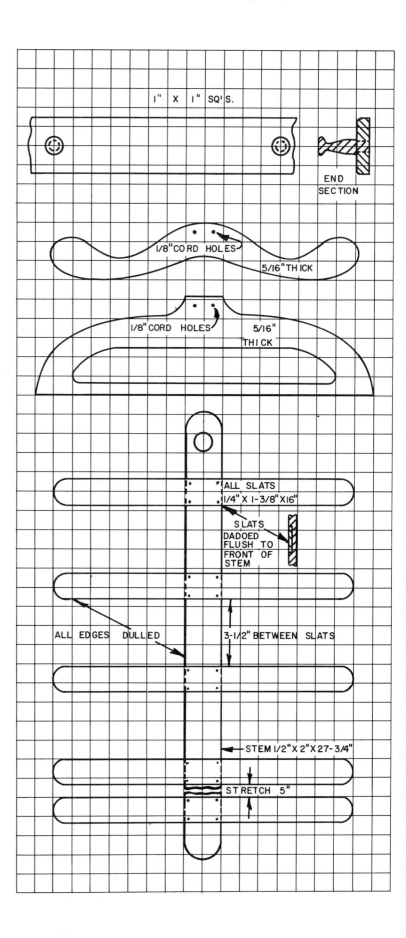

1" X 1" SQ'S.

END
SECTION

1/8"CORD HOLES   5/16"THICK

1/8" CORD HOLES   5/16" THICK

ALL SLATS
1/4" X 1-3/8" X16"

SLATS
DADOED
FLUSH TO
FRONT OF
STEM

ALL EDGES DULLED   3-1/2" BETWEEN SLATS

STEM 1/2" X 2" X 27-3/4"

STRETCH 5"

100

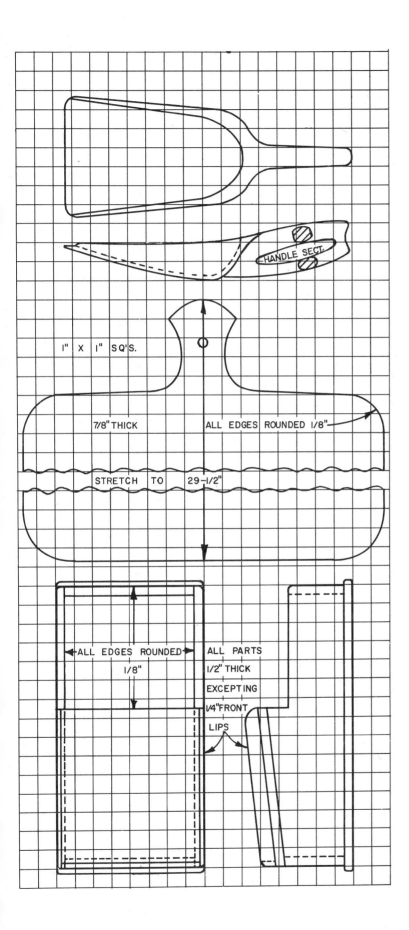

1" X 1" SQ'S.

7/8" THICK · ALL EDGES ROUNDED 1/8"

STRETCH TO 29-1/2"

HANDLE SECT.

←ALL EDGES ROUNDED→ ALL PARTS
1/8" 1/2" THICK
EXCEPTING
1/4" FRONT
LIPS

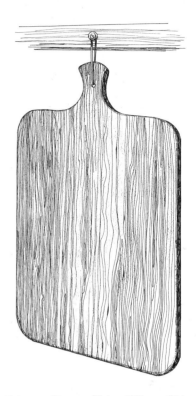

SUGAR SCOOP, Harvard, circa 1830. Fruitlands Museums, Harvard, Mass.

CUTTING BOARD, Union Village, Ohio, circa 1860. Golden Lamb Inn, Lebanon, O.

SCOURING BOX, Union Village, Ohio, circa 1840. Golden Lamb Inn, Lebanon, O.

101

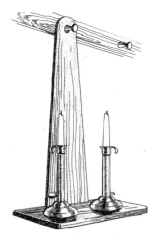

Twin Candle Sconce, Hancock, circa 1830.
Hancock Shaker Village, Hancock, Mass.

Sconce-shelf, Hancock, circa 1830. Hancock
Shaker Village, Hancock, Mass.

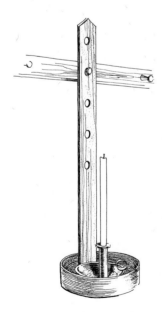

Adjustable Candle Sconce, Union Village,
Ohio, circa 1840. Warren County Historical Museum, Lebanon, O.

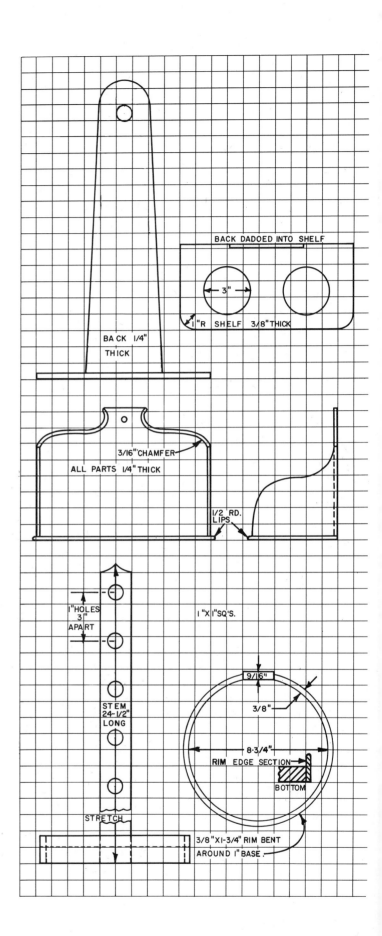

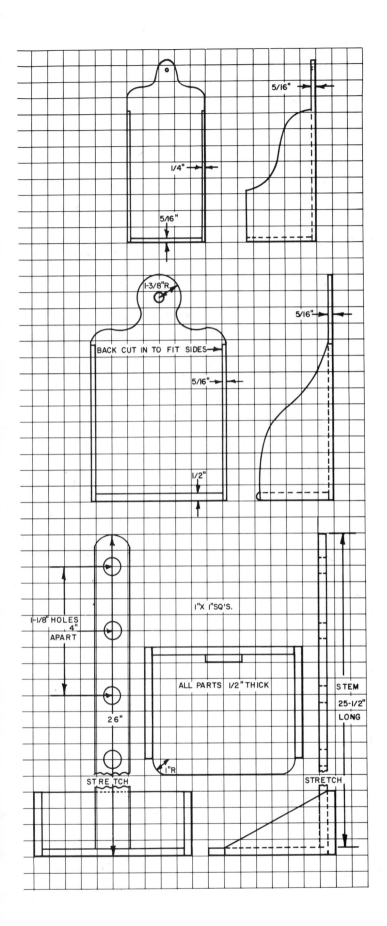

5/16"

1/4"

5/16"

1-3/8"R

5/16"

BACK CUT IN TO FIT SIDES→

5/16"

1/2"

1-1/8" HOLES
4"
APART

1"X 1"SQ'S.

STEM

26"

ALL PARTS 1/2" THICK

25-1/2"

LONG

1"R

STRETCH

STRETCH

PIPE BOX, Sabbathday Lake, Maine, circa 1840. Hancock Shaker Village, Hancock, Mass.

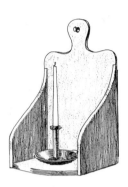

SCONCE, Harvard, circa 1840. Fruitlands Museums, Harvard, Mass.

ADJUSTABLE SCONCE, Kentucky origin; early to mid-nineteenth century.

HAND LOOKING GLASS, Union Village, Ohio, circa 1850. Warren County Historical Museum, Lebanon, O.

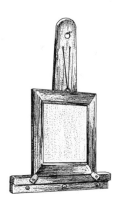

PEGGED HANGER AND SMALL LOOKING GLASS, Harvard, circa 1840. Fruitlands Museums, Harvard, Mass.

LOOKING GLASS ON HANGER, Hancock, circa 1840. Hancock Shaker Village, Hancock, Mass.

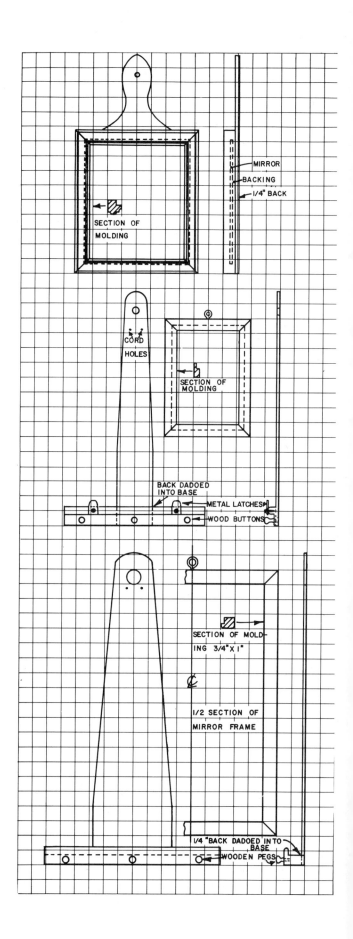

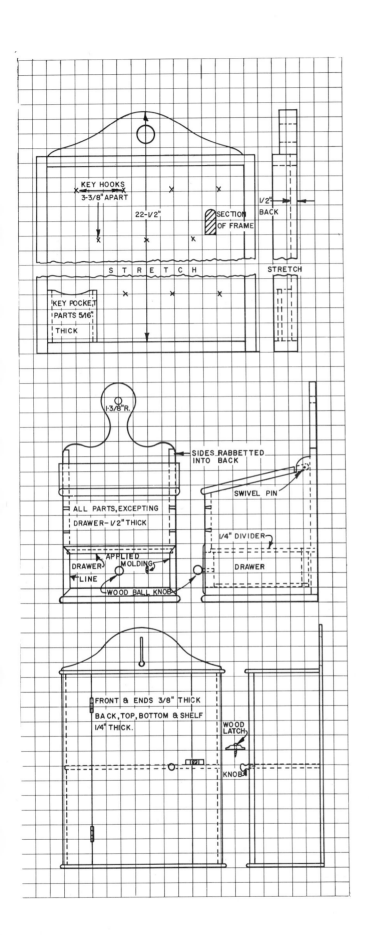

KEY BOARD, New Lebanon, circa 1850. The Shaker Museum, Old Chatham, N.Y.

WALL BOX, Union Village, Ohio, circa 1840. Golden Lamb Inn, Lebanon, O.

WALL CUPBOARD, New Lebanon, circa 1830. Hancock Shaker Village, Hancock, Mass.

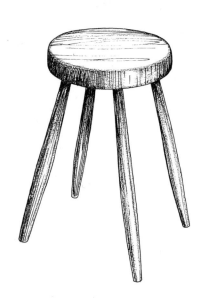

PEG-LEG STOOL, Hancock, circa 1840. Hancock
Shaker Village, Hancock, Mass.

PEG-LEG BENCH, Hancock, circa 1840. Hancock
Shaker Village, Hancock, Mass.

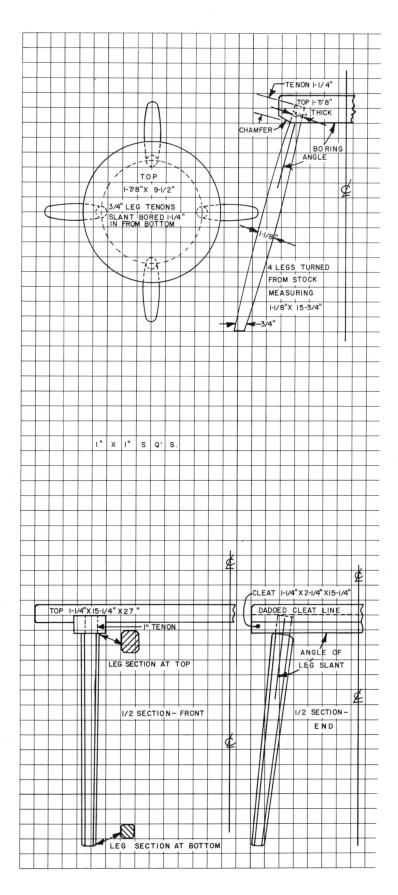

TENON 1-1/4"

TOP 1-7/8"

3/4" THICK

CHAMFER

BORING
ANGLE

TOP
1-7/8" X 9-1/2"

3/4" LEG TENONS
SLANT BORED 1-1/4"
IN FROM BOTTOM

1-1/8"

4 LEGS TURNED
FROM STOCK
MEASURING
1-1/8" X 15-3/4"

3/4"

1" X 1" SQ'S.

CLEAT 1-1/4" X 2-1/4" X 15-1/4"

TOP 1-1/4" X 15-1/4" X 27"

DADOED CLEAT LINE

1" TENON

ANGLE OF
LEG SLANT

LEG SECTION AT TOP

1/2 SECTION— FRONT

1/2 SECTION—
END

LEG SECTION AT BOTTOM

106

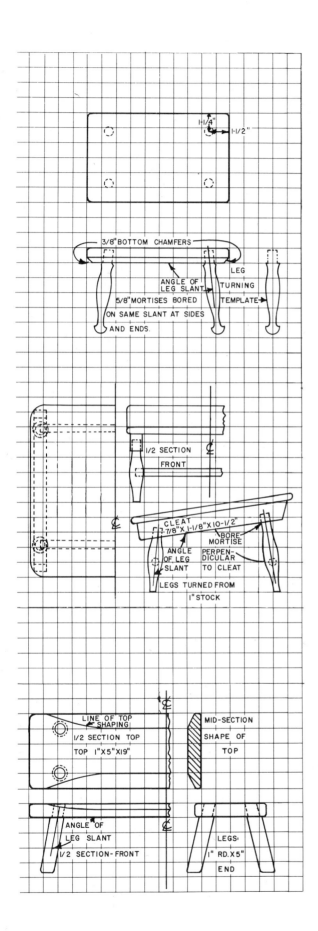

3/8" BOTTOM CHAMFERS

ANGLE OF
LEG SLANT

LEG
TURNING
TEMPLATE

5/8" MORTISES BORED
ON SAME SLANT AT SIDES
AND ENDS.

1/2 SECTION
FRONT

CLEAT
7/8" X 1-1/8" X 10-1/2"

BORE
MORTISE

ANGLE
OF LEG
SLANT

PERPEN-
DICULAR
TO CLEAT

LEGS TURNED FROM
1" STOCK

LINE OF TOP
SHAPING

1/2 SECTION TOP

TOP 1" X 5" X 19"

MID-SECTION

SHAPE OF

TOP

ANGLE OF
LEG SLANT

1/2 SECTION-FRONT

LEGS
1" RD. X 5"

END

FOOTSTOOL, Hancock, circa 1850. Hancock
Shaker Village, Hancock, Mass.

WAGAN CRICKET, New (Mt.) Lebanon, 1873.
The Shaker Museum, Old Chatham, N.Y.

PEG-LEG FOOTSTOOL, New Lebanon, circa 1820.
Hancock Shaker Village, Hancock, Mass.

STEP-CHEST, Canterbury, New Hampshire, circa 1885. The Shaker Museum, Old Chatham, N.Y.

SET OF STEPS, Hancock, circa 1830. Hancock Shaker Village, Hancock, Mass.

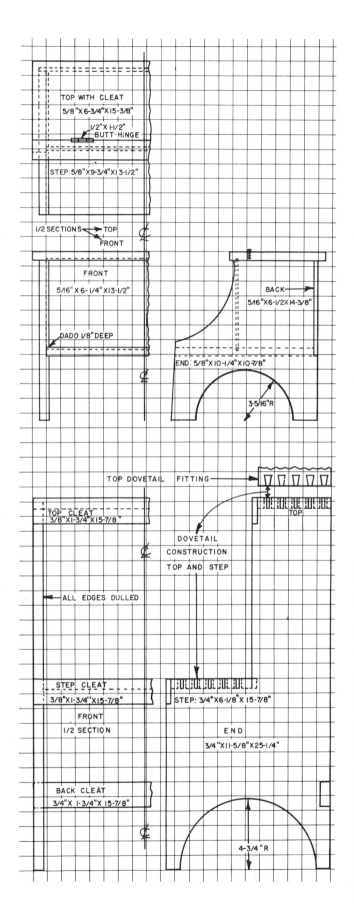

108

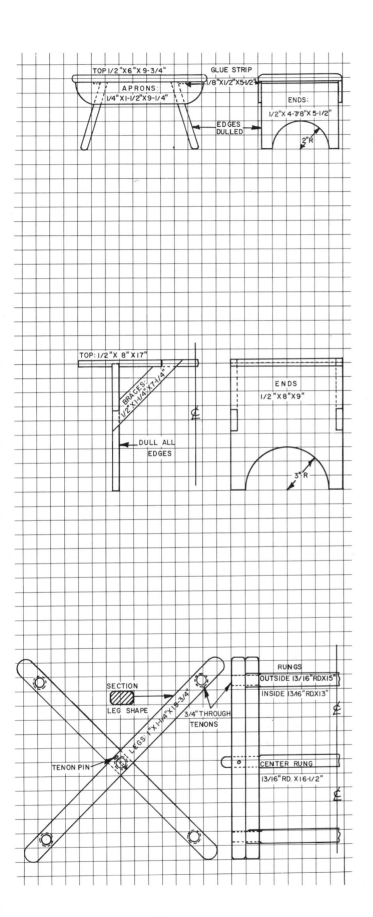

FOOTSTOOL, Hancock, circa 1840. Hancock Shaker Village, Hancock, Mass.

SMALL BENCH, Hancock, circa 1830. The Shaker Museum, Old Chatham, N.Y.

FOLDING STOOL, Sabbathday Lake, Maine. The Shaker Museum, Sabbathday Lake, Me.

SEWING CHEST, Sabbathday Lake, Maine. The Shaker Museum, Sabbathday Lake, Me.

SMALL CHEST, Harvard, circa 1850. Fruitlands Museums, Harvard, Mass.

CASE OF TWO-DRAWERS, Harvard, circa 1850. Fruitlands Museums, Harvard, Mass.

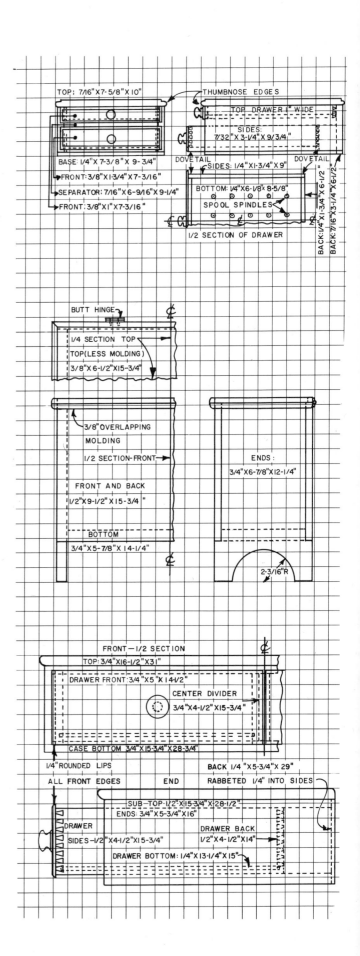

TOP: 7/16"X7-5/8"X10"
THUMBNOSE EDGES
TOP DRAWER 1" WIDE
SIDES: 7/32" X 3-1/4" X 9/3/4"
BASE: 1/4" X 7-3/8" X 9-3/4"
DOVETAIL
SIDES: 1/4"X1-3/4"X9"
DOVETAIL
FRONT: 3/8"X1-3/4"X7-3/16"
BOTTOM: 1/4"X6-1/8"X 8-5/8"
SEPARATOR: 7/16"X6-9/16"X9-1/4"
SPOOL SPINDLES
FRONT: 3/8"X1"X7-3/16"
BACK:1/4"X1-3/4"X 6-1/2"
BACK:7/16"X3-1/4"X6-1/2"
1/2 SECTION OF DRAWER

BUTT HINGE
1/4 SECTION TOP
TOP(LESS MOLDING)
3/8"X 6-1/2"X15-3/4"
3/8"OVERLAPPING MOLDING
1/2 SECTION-FRONT
ENDS: 3/4"X6-7/8"X12-1/4"
FRONT AND BACK
1/2"X9-1/2"X15-3/4"
BOTTOM
3/4"X5-7/8"X 14-1/4"
2-3/16"R

FRONT—1/2 SECTION
TOP: 3/4"X16-1/2"X31"
DRAWER FRONT: 3/4"X5"X 14-1/2"
CENTER DIVIDER 3/4"X4-1/2"X15-3/4"
CASE BOTTOM 3/4"X15-3/4"X28-3/4"
1/4"ROUNDED LIPS
BACK 1/4"X5-3/4"X 29"
ALL FRONT EDGES
END
RABBETED 1/4" INTO SIDES
SUB-TOP-1/2"X15-3/4"X 28-1/2"
ENDS: 3/4"X5-3/4"X16
DRAWER
SIDES—1/2"X4-1/2"X15-3/4"
DRAWER BACK 1/2"X4-1/2"X14"
DRAWER BOTTOM: 1/4"X13-1/4"X15"

110

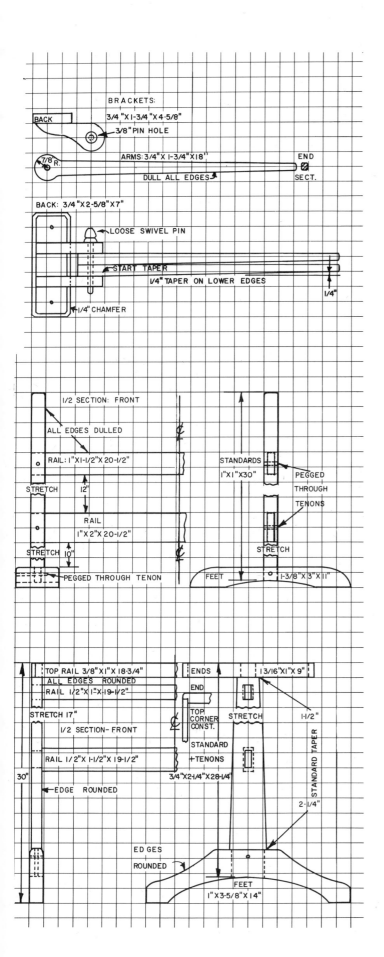

BRACKETS:

BACK
3/4"X 1-3/4"X 4-5/8"

3/8" PIN HOLE

7/8" R.
ARMS: 3/4"X 1-3/4"X 18"
DULL ALL EDGES

END
SECT.

BACK: 3/4"X 2-5/8"X 7"

LOOSE SWIVEL PIN

START TAPER

1/4" TAPER ON LOWER EDGES

1/4"

1/4" CHAMFER

1/2 SECTION: FRONT

ALL EDGES DULLED

RAIL: 1"X 1-1/2"X 20-1/2"

STANDARDS
1"X 1"X 30"

PEGGED

STRETCH

THROUGH

12"

TENONS

RAIL
1"X 2"X 20-1/2"

STRETCH

10"

STRETCH

PEGGED THROUGH TENON

FEET

1-3/8"X 3"X 11"

TOP RAIL 3/8"X 1"X 18-3/4"

ENDS

13/16"X 1"X 9"

ALL EDGES ROUNDED

END

RAIL 1/2"X 1"X 19-1/2"

STRETCH 17"

TOP
CORNER
CONST.

STRETCH

1-1/2"

1/2 SECTION- FRONT

STANDARD
+TENONS

RAIL 1/2"X 1-1/2"X 19-1/2"

3/4"X 2-1/4"X 28-1/4"

30"

EDGE ROUNDED

STANDARD TAPER

2-1/4"

EDGES

ROUNDED

FEET
1"X 3-5/8"X 14"

TOWEL RACK, New Lebanon, circa 1850. The Shaker Museum, Old Chatham, N.Y.

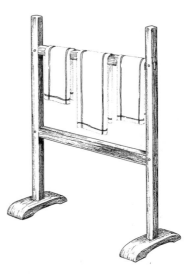

DRYING RACK, Harvard, circa 1840. Fruitlands Museums, Harvard, Mass.

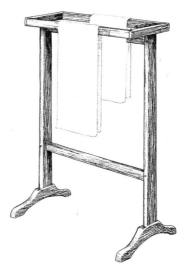

DRYING STAND, Hancock, circa 1850. The Shaker Museum, Sabbathday Lake, Me.

111

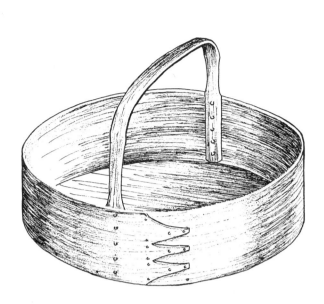

OVAL CARRIER, Harvard, Massachusetts, circa 1840. Fruitlands Museums, Harvard, Mass.

DUST BOX, Hancock, circa 1840. Hancock Shaker Village, Hancock, Mass.

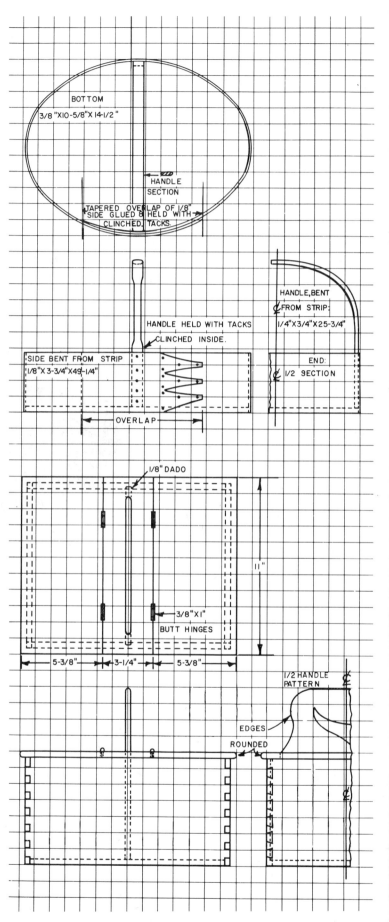

BOTTOM
3/8"X10-5/8"X 14-1/2"

HANDLE SECTION

TAPERED OVERLAP OF 1/8"
SIDE GLUED & HELD WITH
CLINCHED TACKS.

HANDLE HELD WITH TACKS
CLINCHED INSIDE.

HANDLE, BENT
FROM STRIP:
1/4"X3/4"X25-3/4"

SIDE BENT FROM STRIP
1/8"X 3-3/4"X49-1/4"

END:
1/2 SECTION

OVERLAP

1/8" DADO

3/8"X1"

BUTT HINGES

11"

5-3/8"   3-1/4"   5-3/8"

1/2 HANDLE
PATTERN

EDGES
ROUNDED

CHAPTER VI

SHAKER
UTILITY
DESIGNS
with Museum-Measured Drawings

DOVETAILED DOUGH BIN

This beautifully crafted pumpkin-pine dough bin was made either at Hancock or New Lebanon around the middle of the nineteenth century. Its precise proportions and sturdy dovetailed construction make it as strong and serviceable today as it was when first used by Shaker bakers over a century ago. *Photographed courtesy the Shaker Museum, Old Chatham, N.Y.*

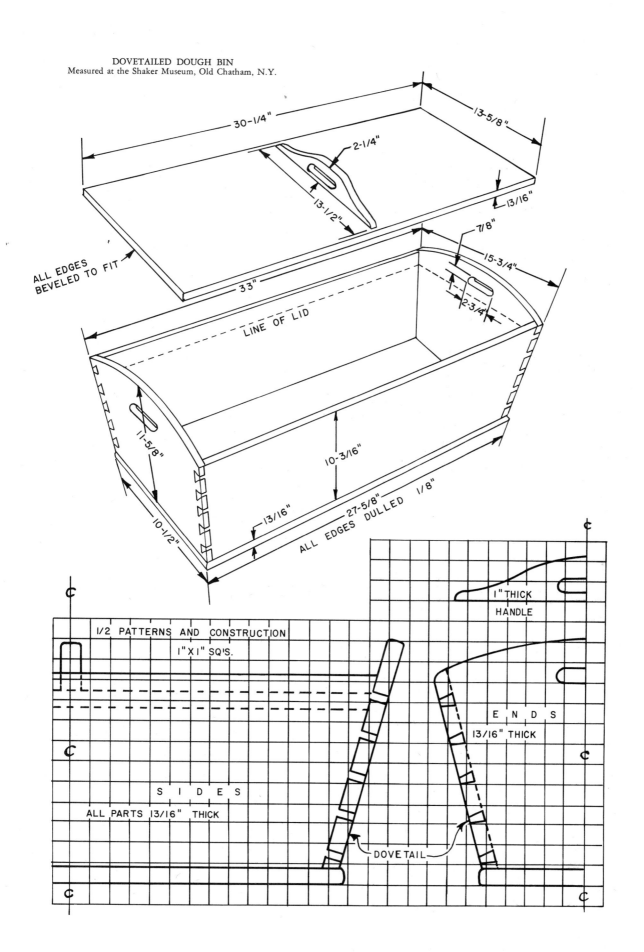

DOVETAILED DOUGH BIN
Measured at the Shaker Museum, Old Chatham, N.Y.

30-1/4"

13-5/8"

2-1/4"

13-1/2"

13/16"

ALL EDGES BEVELED TO FIT

7/8"

15-3/4"

33"

LINE OF LID

2-3/4"

11-5/8"

10-3/16"

10-1/2"

13/16"

27-5/8"

ALL EDGES DULLED 1/8"

1/2 PATTERNS AND CONSTRUCTION
1" X 1" SQ'S.

1" THICK
HANDLE

E N D S
13/16" THICK

S I D E S

ALL PARTS 13/16" THICK

DOVETAIL

BUTCHER BLOCK

The massive Shaker butcher block was made by mounting a section of sycamore tree trunk on three turned legs. It was made about 1850 at Pleasant Hill, Kentucky. The wood was so carefully cured that the top remains undamaged after more than a century of hard use. *Photographed courtesy the Shaker Museum, Old Chatham, N.Y.*

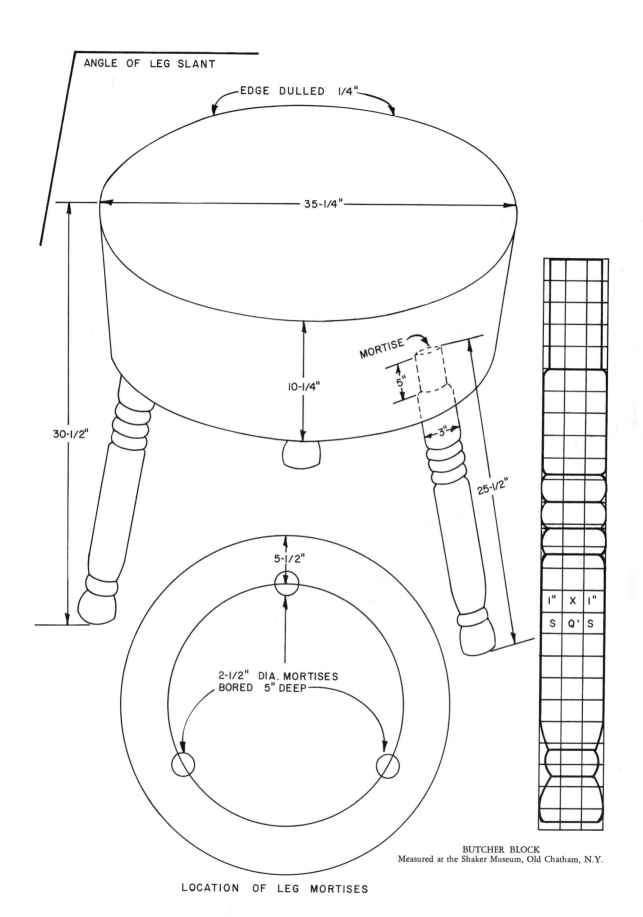

ANGLE OF LEG SLANT

EDGE DULLED 1/4"

35-1/4"

10-1/4"

30-1/2"

MORTISE

5"

3"

25-1/2"

5-1/2"

2-1/2" DIA. MORTISES
BORED 5" DEEP

LOCATION OF LEG MORTISES

1" X 1"
S Q'S

BUTCHER BLOCK
Measured at the Shaker Museum, Old Chatham, N.Y.

117

LOG BIN

This spacious wood bin was built at New Lebanon, New York, around 1830. The sturdy details of its construction would seldom be found in similar utility items made outside the Shaker communities. Observe how the top drying rack is advantageously mounted to receive the heat of an adjoining Shaker stove. *Photographed by Lees Studio courtesy the Shaker Museum, Old Chatham, N.Y.*

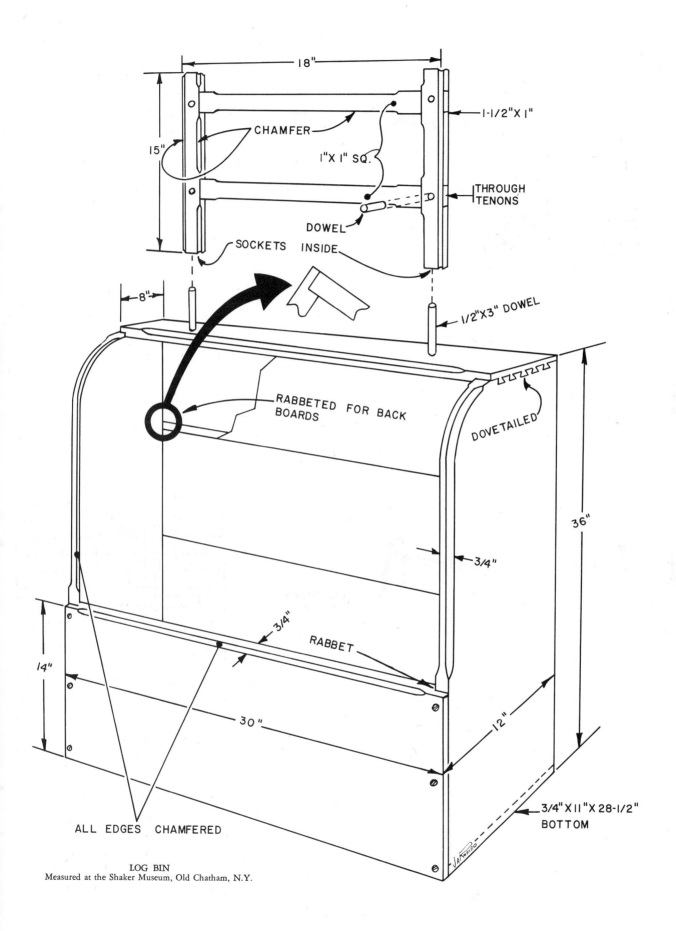

18"

CHAMFER

15"

1"X 1" SQ.

1-1/2"X 1"

THROUGH TENONS

DOWEL

SOCKETS INSIDE

8"

1/2"X3" DOWEL

RABBETED FOR BACK BOARDS

DOVETAILED

36"

3/4"

3/4"

RABBET

14"

30"

12"

ALL EDGES CHAMFERED

3/4"X 11"X 28-1/2" BOTTOM

LOG BIN
Measured at the Shaker Museum, Old Chatham, N.Y.

SET OF SHELVES

Simple utility shelves were made for all living and working areas of Shaker dwellings. Usually they contained the personal effects or working requirements of individual members of the community. This is a typical nineteenth-century Hancock design. *Photographed courtesy Hancock Shaker Village, Hancock, Mass.*

SET OF SHELVES
Measured at Hancock Shaker Village, Hancock, Mass.

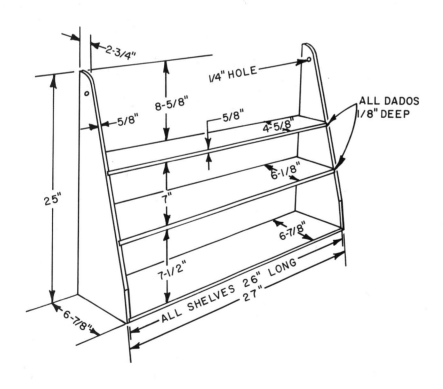

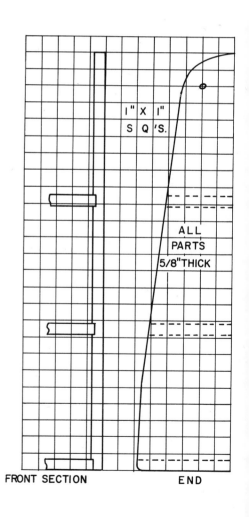

FRONT SECTION   END

HANGING DISH SHELVES

These large hanging shelves were used by the North Family of New Lebanon around 1830. They were designed to fit flush beneath the pegboard wall trim. Metal rod reinforcement of the bottom shelf held the parts snugly together and prevented the shelves from bending under heavy loads. *Photographed courtesy Hancock Shaker Village, Hancock, Mass.*

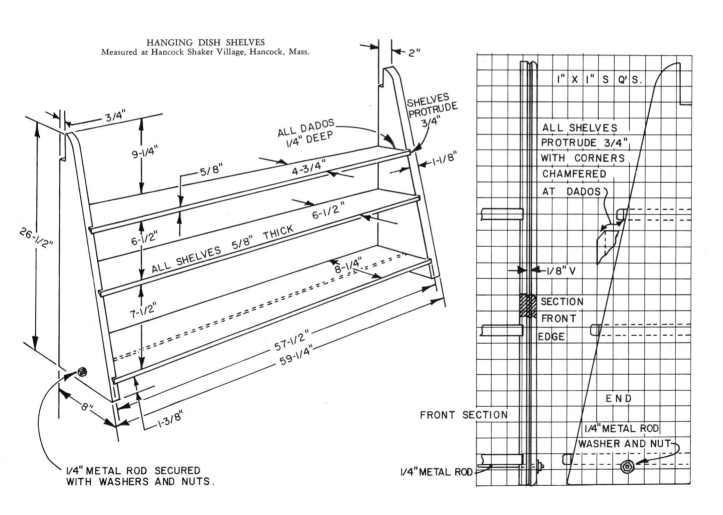

HANGING DISH SHELVES
Measured at Hancock Shaker Village, Hancock, Mass.

2"

SHELVES PROTRUDE 3/4"

ALL DADOS 1/4" DEEP

3/4"

9-1/4"

5/8"   4-3/4"   1-1/8"

6-1/2"   6-1/2"

ALL SHELVES 5/8" THICK

26-1/2"

7-1/2"   8-1/4"

57-1/2"
59-1/4"

8"

1-3/8"

1/4" METAL ROD SECURED WITH WASHERS AND NUTS.

1" X 1" SQ'S.

ALL SHELVES PROTRUDE 3/4" WITH CORNERS CHAMFERED AT DADOS

1/8" V

SECTION FRONT EDGE

END

FRONT SECTION

1/4" METAL ROD

1/4" METAL ROD WASHER AND NUT

121

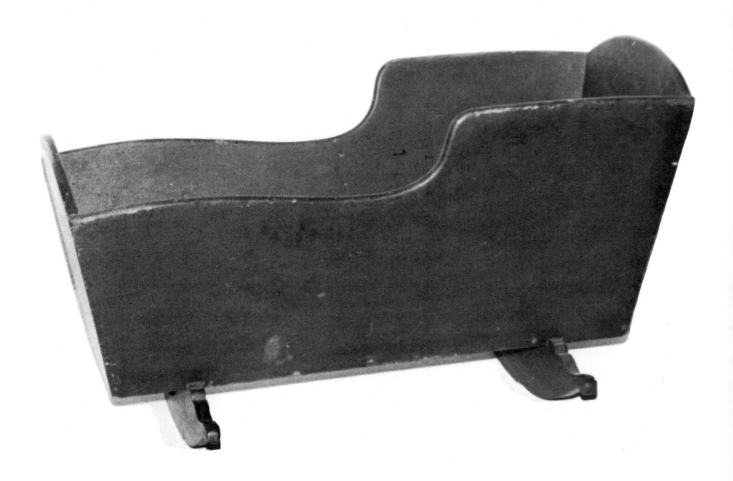

CRADLE

One may wonder what the celibate Shakers would be doing with an infant's cradle. The fact is that foundling infants and the children of converts were part of the Shaker communities. This cradle of pumpkin pine was built at New Lebanon around 1840. *Photographed courtesy the Shaker Museum, Old Chatham, N.Y.*

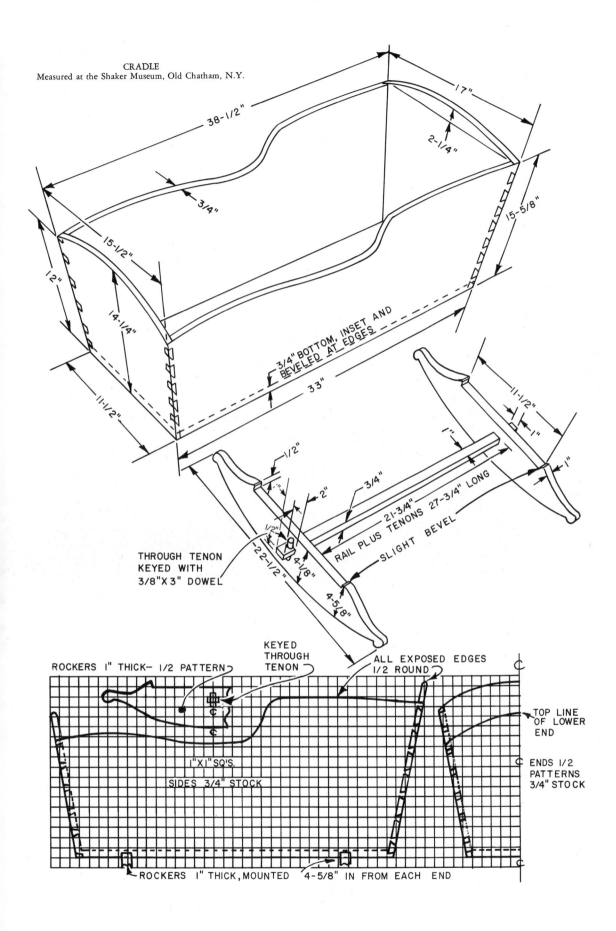

CRADLE
Measured at the Shaker Museum, Old Chatham, N.Y.

38-1/2"

17"

2-1/4"

3/4"

15-5/8"

15-1/2"

12"

14-1/4"

3/4" BOTTOM, INSET AND
BEVELED AT EDGES

11-1/2"

33"

11-1/2"

1"

1/2"

2"

3/4"

1"

21-3/4"

RAIL PLUS TENONS 27-3/4" LONG

SLIGHT BEVEL

1/2"

4-1/8"

22-1/2"

THROUGH TENON
KEYED WITH
3/8"X 3" DOWEL

4-5/8"

KEYED
THROUGH
TENON

ALL EXPOSED EDGES
1/2 ROUND

ROCKERS 1" THICK- 1/2 PATTERN

TOP LINE
OF LOWER
END

1"X1" SQ'S.
SIDES 3/4" STOCK

ENDS 1/2
PATTERNS
3/4" STOCK

ROCKERS 1" THICK, MOUNTED 4-5/8" IN FROM EACH END

123

HANCOCK BENCH

These beautifully crafted little benches were first built at Hancock, Massachusetts, around 1830. Note the cross-lap notching of legs and apron braces, which provided ample strength while at the same time reducing the overall bulk and weight. *Photographed courtesy Hancock Shaker Village, Hancock, Mass.*

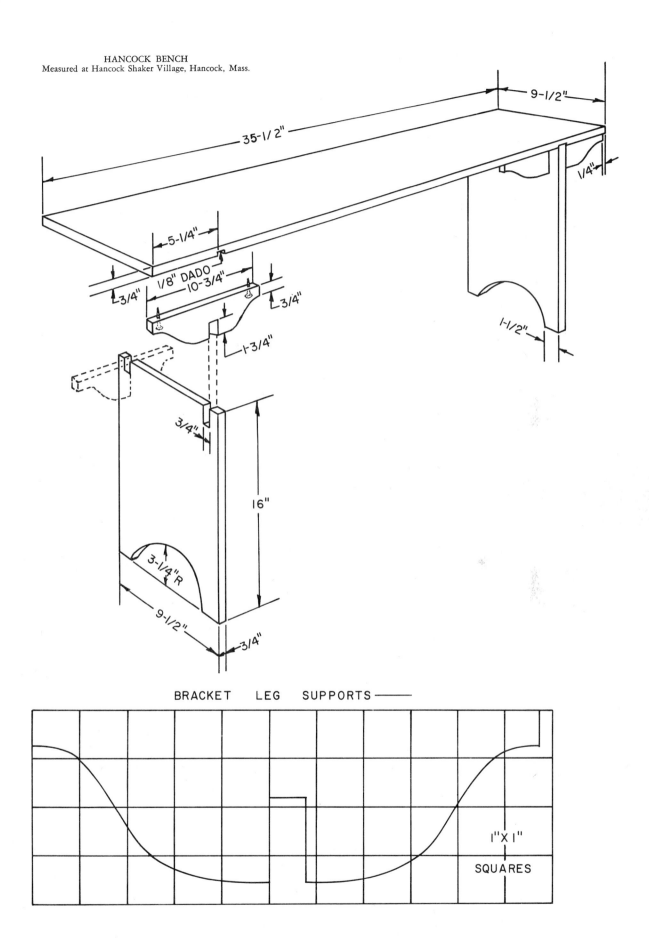

BRACKET LEG SUPPORTS ——

1" X 1" SQUARES

MEETING HOUSE BENCH

Even the simplest benches built by the Shakers were more cleverly constructed than those made in the world outside. The meeting house bench, built at New Lebanon around 1820, used lighter parts (to make it easier to move) but reinforced their construction with haunched, half-dovetailed braces. As a result, this bench is as strong and sturdy today as it was a century and a half ago. *Photographed by Lees Studio courtesy the Shaker Museum, Old Chatham, N.Y.*

126

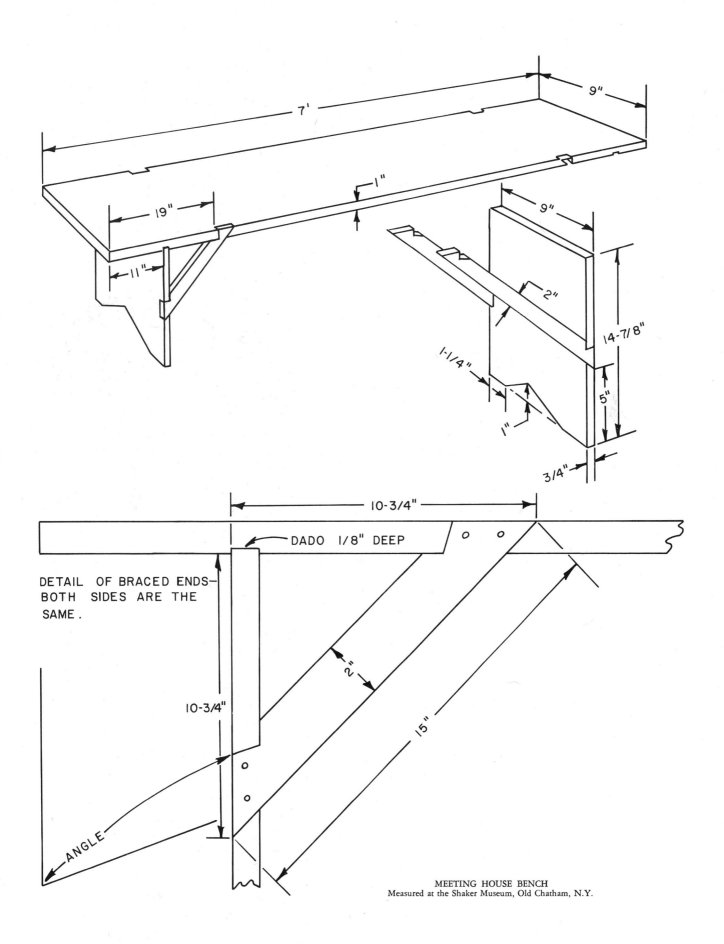

7'

9"

19"

1"

9"

11"

2"

14-7/8"

1-1/4"

5"

1"

3/4"

10-3/4"

DADO 1/8" DEEP

DETAIL OF BRACED ENDS—
BOTH SIDES ARE THE
SAME.

10-3/4"

2"

15"

ANGLE

MEETING HOUSE BENCH
Measured at the Shaker Museum, Old Chatham, N.Y.

UTILITY BENCH

The peg-leg utility bench, of early origin, was rigged with a hand roller which was used by the Shaker Sisters to roll glued poplar wood and palm fiber to a cambric base in the process of making their distinctive Shaker bonnets. *Photographed courtesy the Shaker Museum, Old Chatham, N.Y.*

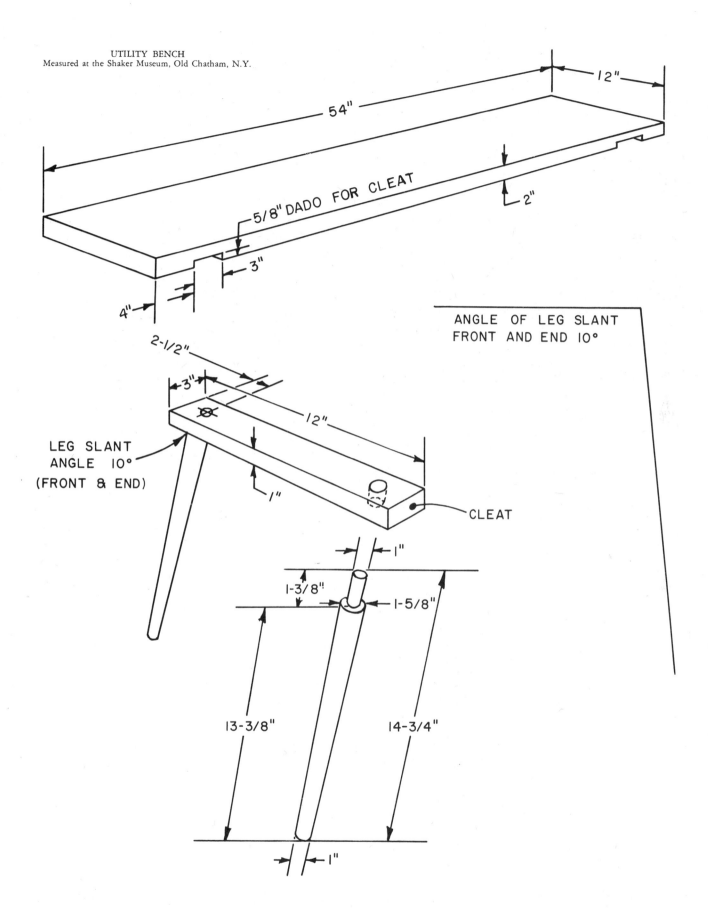

UTILITY BENCH
Measured at the Shaker Museum, Old Chatham, N.Y.

54"

12"

5/8" DADO FOR CLEAT

2"

3"

4"

2-1/2"

3"

ANGLE OF LEG SLANT
FRONT AND END 10°

12"

LEG SLANT
ANGLE 10°
(FRONT & END)

1"

CLEAT

1"

1-3/8"

1-5/8"

13-3/8"

14-3/4"

1"

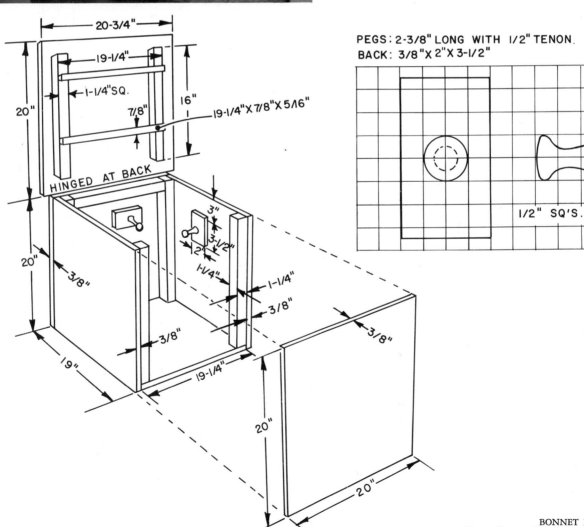

PEGS: 2-3/8" LONG WITH 1/2" TENON.
BACK: 3/8"X 2"X 3-1/2"

20-3/4"

19-1/4"

1-1/4"SQ.

7/8"

16"

19-1/4"X 7/8"X 5/16"

20"

HINGED AT BACK

3"

3-1/2"

2"

1-1/4"

20"

3/8"

3/8"

19"

19-1/4"

1-1/4"

3/8"

3/8"

20"

20"

1/2" SQ'S.

BONNET BOX
Measured at the Shaker Museum, Old Chatham, N.Y.

130

BONNET BOX AND STORAGE BOX

Boxes of assorted sizes and types were produced in abundance by Shaker craftsmen. The pine bonnet box, shown on facing page, was made at New Lebanon around 1820. It was used to carry the distinctive bonnets worn by Shaker Eldresses during their travels between communities. Pegs on the inside kept the bonnets separated to avoid crushing the hard crowns. Storage boxes, like the one at the right, were delicately dovetailed and flawlessly fitted. They were used to store personal effects and tools. Because of their religious faith and trust, the Shakers seldom fitted their boxes and chests with locks. *Photographed courtesy the Shaker Museum, Old Chatham, N.Y.*

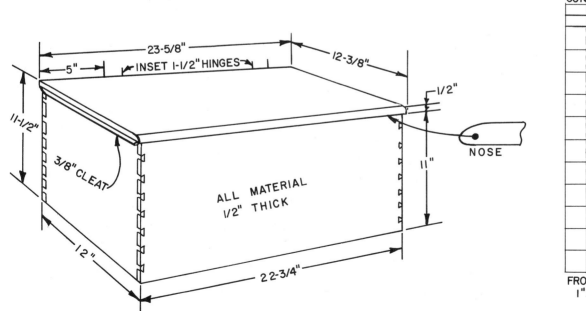

STORAGE BOX
Measured at the Shaker Museum, Old Chatham, N.Y.

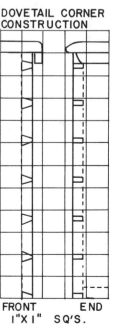

KITCHEN TABLE

The sturdy kitchen cutting table was used by the South Family at New Lebanon, around 1830. With its special cutter and heavy cutting board it served to slice quantities of Shaker baked bread for the many members of the community. *Photographed courtesy Hancock Shaker Village, Hancock, Mass.*

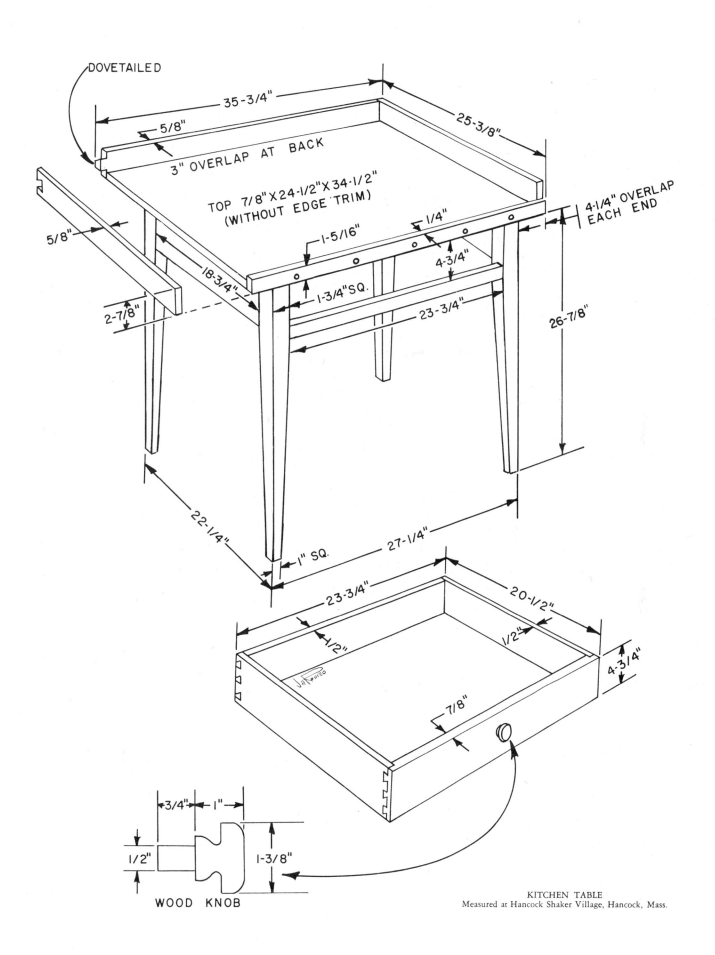

DOVETAILED

35-3/4"

5/8"

3" OVERLAP AT BACK

25-3/8"

TOP 7/8" X 24-1/2" X 34-1/2"
(WITHOUT EDGE TRIM)

1/4"

4-1/4" OVERLAP
EACH END

1-5/16"

5/8"

4-3/4"

18-3/4"

1-3/4" SQ.

23-3/4"

26-7/8"

2-7/8"

22-1/4"

1" SQ.

27-1/4"

23-3/4"

20-1/2"

1/2"

1/2"

4-3/4"

7/8"

3/4"   1"

1/2"

1-3/8"

WOOD KNOB

KITCHEN TABLE
Measured at Hancock Shaker Village, Hancock, Mass.

133

WALL CUPBOARD

Spacious Shaker wall cupboards were made with the same painstaking attention to details of craftsmanship as the finer furniture of domestic use. This cupboard, which was built by the Harvard Shakers around 1840, has neatly pegged mortise and tenon joints and softly shaped edge molding; it displays excellent proportioning of parts. *Photographed courtesy Fruitlands Museums, Harvard, Mass.*

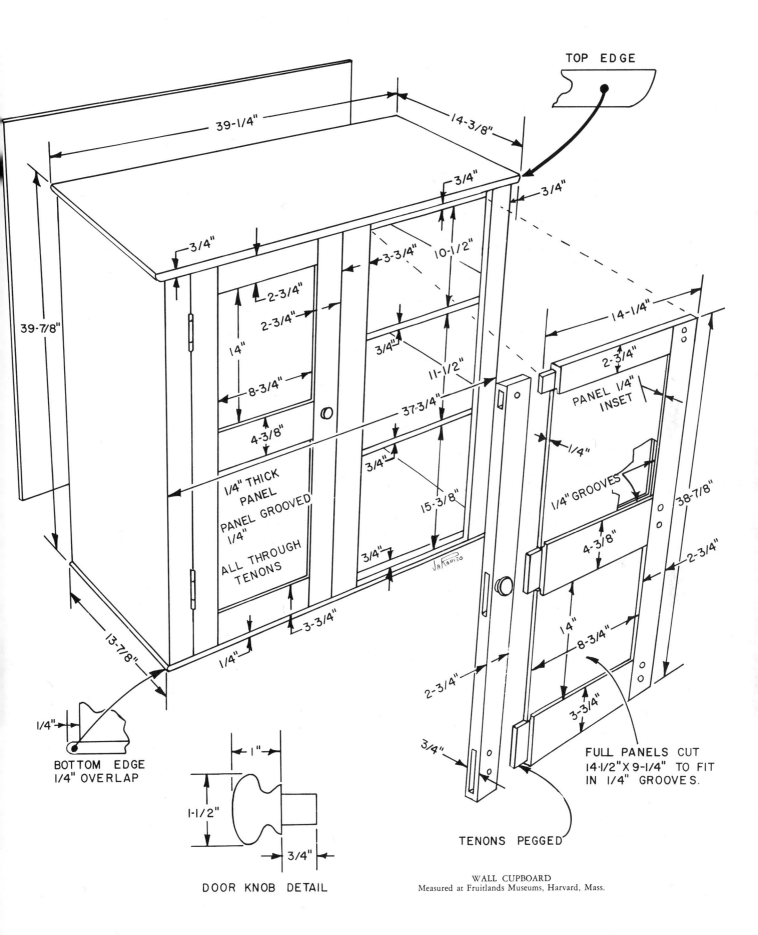

TOP EDGE

39-1/4"

14-3/8"

3/4"

3/4"

39-7/8"

3/4"

3-3/4"

10-1/2"

2-3/4"

2-3/4"

14"

3/4"

8-3/4"

11-1/2"

37-3/4"

4-3/8"

1/4" THICK
PANEL

PANEL GROOVED
1/4"

ALL THROUGH
TENONS

3/4"

15-3/8"

3/4"

14-1/4"

2-3/4"

PANEL 1/4"
INSET

1/4"

1/4" GROOVES

38-7/8"

2-3/4"

14"

8-3/4"

3/4"

3-3/4"

1/4"

3-3/4"

13-7/8"

1/4"

2-3/4"

3/4"

FULL PANELS CUT
14-1/2" X 9-1/4" TO FIT
IN 1/4" GROOVES.

1/4"

BOTTOM EDGE
1/4" OVERLAP

1"

1-1/2"

3/4"

DOOR KNOB DETAIL

TENONS PEGGED

WALL CUPBOARD
Measured at Fruitlands Museums, Harvard, Mass.

135

DRY SINK

With our modern kitchen plumbing it may be hard to realize that people depended on solidly built wooden dry sinks, before our gleaming facilities with hot and cold running water came along. But the Shaker dry sinks were much more handsome! This beautifully crafted combination of trough and cupboard was built by the Harvard Shakers around 1850. That gadget at the right is a Shaker sausage stuffer. *Photographed courtesy Fruitlands Museums, Harvard, Mass.*

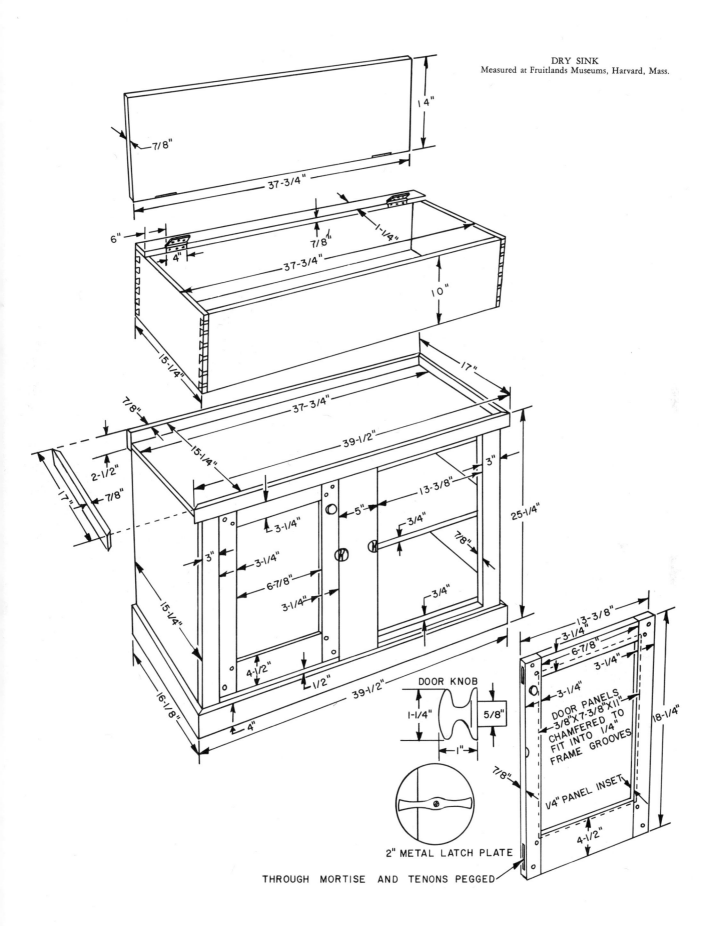

DRY SINK
Measured at Fruitlands Museums, Harvard, Mass.

1 4"

7/8"

37-3/4"

6"

4"

7/8"

1-1/4"

37-3/4"

10"

15-1/4"

17"

7/8"

37-3/4"

15-1/4"

39-1/2"

3"

2-1/2"

17"

7/8"

13-3/8"

25-1/4"

3-1/4"

5"

3/4"

7/8"

3"

3-1/4"

6-7/8"

3-1/4"

3/4"

15-1/4"

4-1/2"

1/2"

39-1/2"

16-1/8"

4"

DOOR KNOB

1-1/4"

5/8"

1"

13-3/8"

3-1/4"

6-7/8"

3-1/4"

3-1/4"

DOOR PANELS
3/8"X7-3/8"X11"
CHAMFERED TO
FIT INTO 1/4"
FRAME GROOVES

18-1/4"

7/8"

1/4" PANEL INSET

4-1/2"

2" METAL LATCH PLATE

THROUGH MORTISE AND TENONS PEGGED

137

KITCHEN DESK-CUPBOARD

The utility desk-cupboard of pumpkin pine was built at Hancock around 1830. It provided plenty of space for keeping the records and accouterments of communal kitchen accounting. After the paper work was finished, the drop-leaf writing counter could be folded up flush to the front. *Photographed courtesy Hancock Shaker Village, Hancock, Mass.*

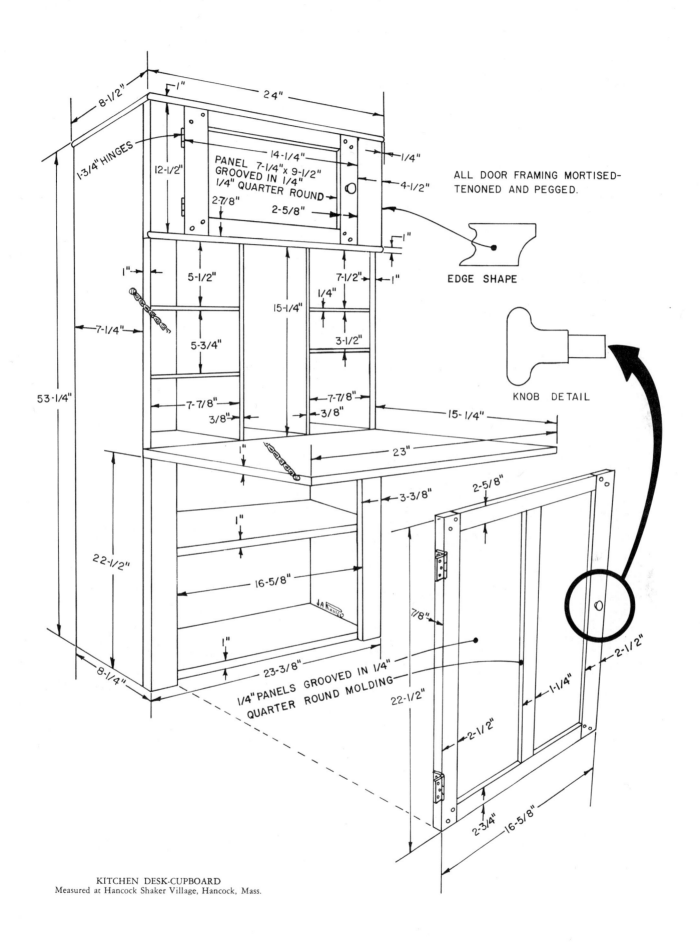

ALL DOOR FRAMING MORTISED-
TENONED AND PEGGED.

EDGE SHAPE

KNOB DETAIL

PANEL 7-1/4" x 9-1/2"
GROOVED IN 1/4"
1/4" QUARTER ROUND

1/4" PANELS GROOVED IN 1/4"
QUARTER ROUND MOLDING

KITCHEN DESK-CUPBOARD
Measured at Hancock Shaker Village, Hancock, Mass.

139

FLIGHT OF SHELVES

More than a hundred years after the Hancock Shakers first fabricated their "flight of shelves," contemporary designers took notice and started designing shelving systems along similar lines. These utility shelves, of graduated widths, were used by the Shakers for storing canned goods and dairy products. *Photographed courtesy Hancock Shaker Village, Hancock, Mass.*

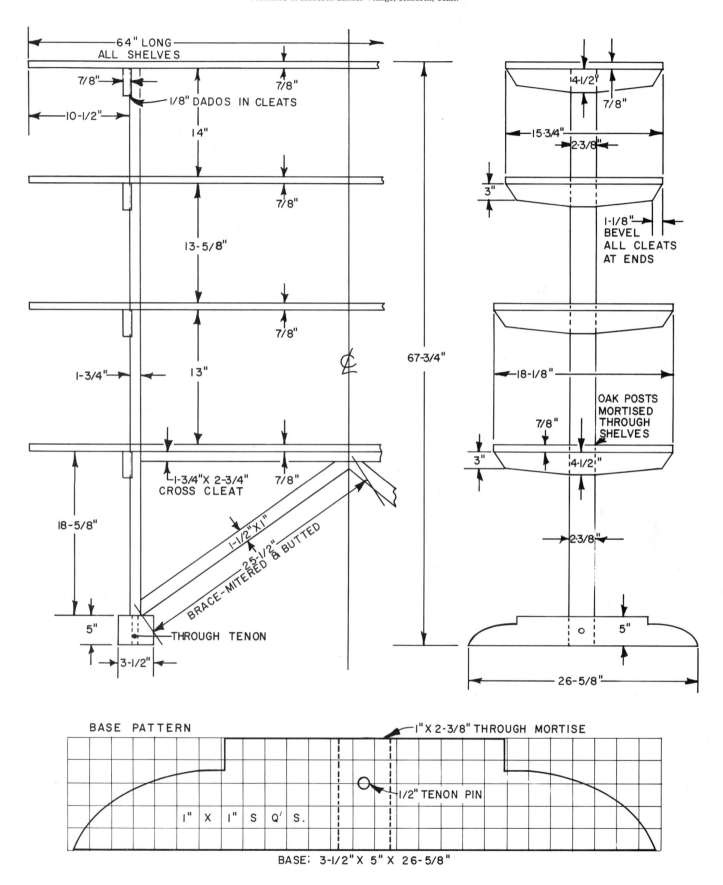

BASE PATTERN

1" X 2-3/8" THROUGH MORTISE

1/2" TENON PIN

1" X 1" SQ' S.

BASE: 3-1/2" X 5" X 26-5/8"

141

UTILITY PEDESTAL

This utility stand, which was made either at Hancock or New Lebanon early in the nineteenth century, could be used as a candlestand, as a reading stand, or as a side table in a Shaker dormitory. It is about the most rudimentary of the Shaker pedestal designs. As shown on the measured drawing, the stem is simply chamfered and angle-bored to receive the three peg legs. *Photographed courtesy the Shaker Museum, Old Chatham, N.Y.*

UTILITY PEDESTAL
Measured at the Shaker Museum, Old Chatham, N.Y.

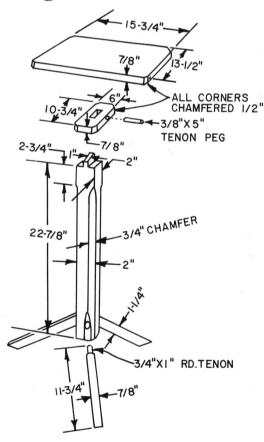

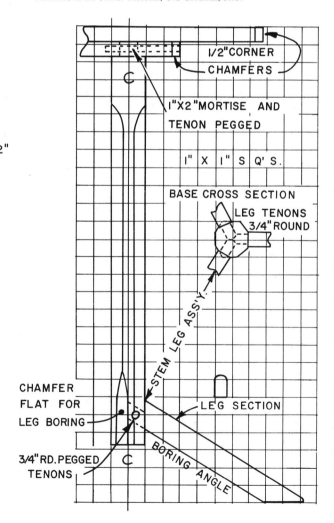

SORTING STAND

This simple Shaker stand was designed to facilitate the sorting of seeds. The top rim, which forms a lip a quarter of an inch above the surface, is scooped down flush at one spot for drawing off the rejected seeds. This pedestal was built by the Shakers of New Lebanon, circa 1840. *Photographed courtesy Hancock Shaker Village, Hancock, Mass.*

SORTING STAND
Measured at Hancock Shaker Village, Hancock, Mass.

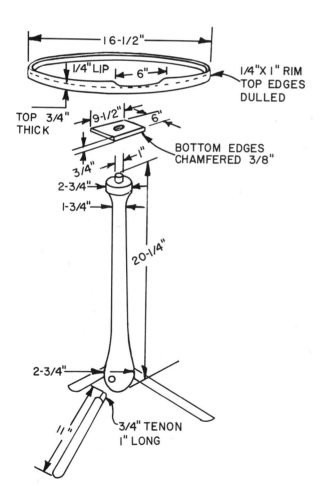

16-1/2"
1/4" LIP
6"
1/4"X1" RIM TOP EDGES DULLED
TOP 3/4" THICK
9-1/2"
6"
BOTTOM EDGES CHAMFERED 3/8"
3/4"
1"
2-3/4"
1-3/4"
20-1/4"
2-3/4"
3/4" TENON 1" LONG
11"

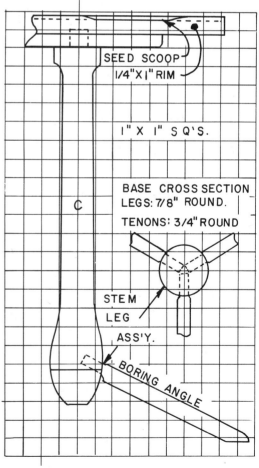

SEED SCOOP
1/4"X1" RIM
1" X 1" SQ'S.
C
BASE CROSS SECTION
LEGS: 7/8" ROUND.
TENONS: 3/4" ROUND
STEM
LEG
ASS'Y.
BORING ANGLE

143

FIREWOOD CARRIER

Even the most commonplace utility items, such as wood carriers, were skillfully constructed by Shaker craftsmen. This ironbound example was built at New Lebanon around 1840. It is probably just as strong and serviceable today as it was when it first emerged from the craftsman's workshop. *Photographed courtesy Hancock Shaker Village, Hancock, Mass.*

FIREWOOD CARRIER
Measured at Hancock Shaker Village, Hancock, Mass.

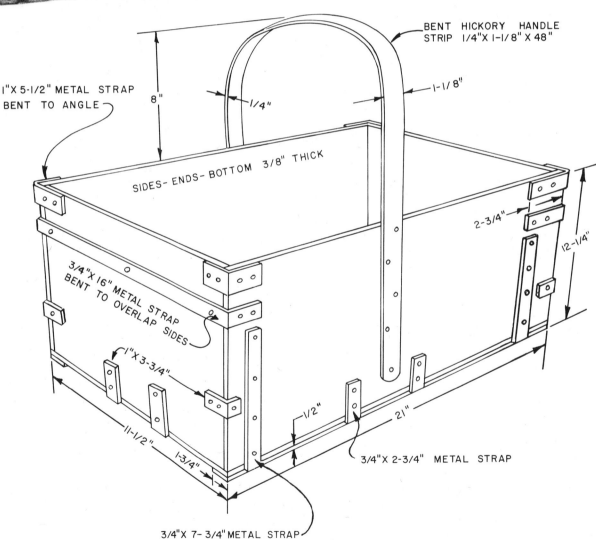

CHAPTER VII

SHAKER FURNITURE CLASSICS

SEWING TABLE

Various types of sewing tables, sewing stands, sewing desks, and sewing chests were built by the Shakers of both eastern and western communities. The design illustrated, which is believed to have been built at Hancock around the middle of the nineteenth century, is nicely proportioned and beautifully constructed. The drop-leaf at the back was extended for cutting and laying out the work. *Photographed courtesy the Shaker Museum, Old Chatham, N.Y.*

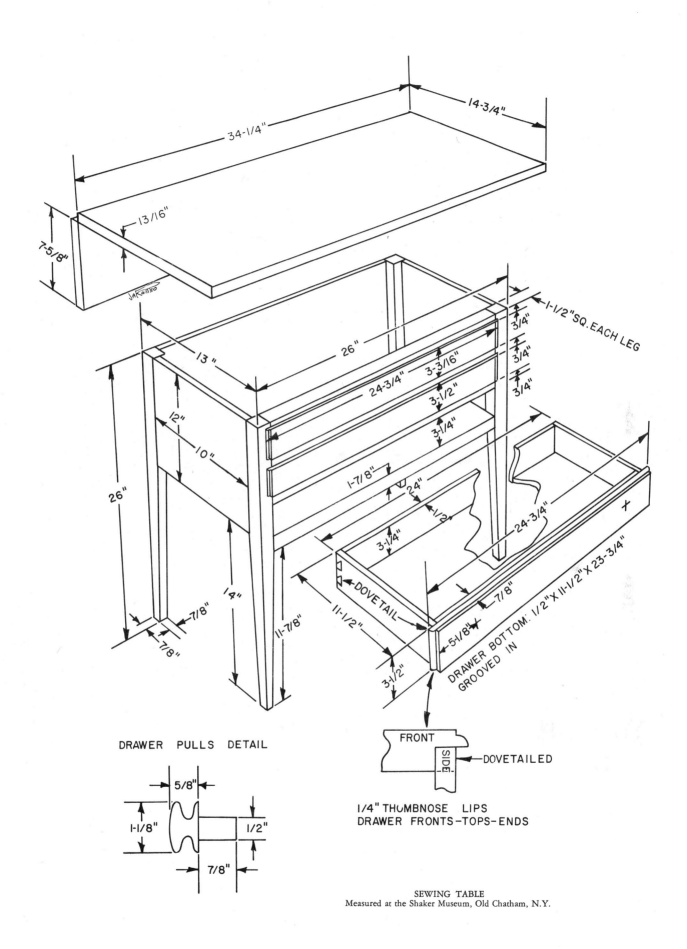

34-1/4"

14-3/4"

13/16"

7-5/8"

JaKaittso

1-1/2" SQ. EACH LEG

3/4"
3/4"
3/4"

13"

26"

3-3/16"

24-3/4"

3-1/2"

12"

10"

3/4"

26"

1-7/8"

24"

1/2"

3-1/4"

24-3/4"

14"

7/8"

11-7/8"

7/8"
7/8"

DOVETAIL

11-1/2"

7/8"

DRAWER BOTTOM: 1/2" X 11-1/2" X 23-3/4"
GROOVED IN

5-1/8"

3-1/2"

DRAWER PULLS DETAIL

5/8"

1-1/8"

1/2"

7/8"

FRONT

SIDE

DOVETAILED

1/4" THUMBNOSE LIPS
DRAWER FRONTS–TOPS–ENDS

SEWING TABLE
Measured at the Shaker Museum, Old Chatham, N.Y.

TURNED TRESTLE TABLE

Distinctive features which most Shaker trestle tables shared in common was their elevation of the central supporting rail to fasten beneath the top, and the arched shaping of their feet. With this construction, the rail did not obstruct the knees of those seated beside the table — and those seated at the ends could tuck their toes under the arched feet. This handsome maple table was made at Hancock around 1830. *Photographed courtesy the Shaker Museum, Old Chatham, N.Y.*

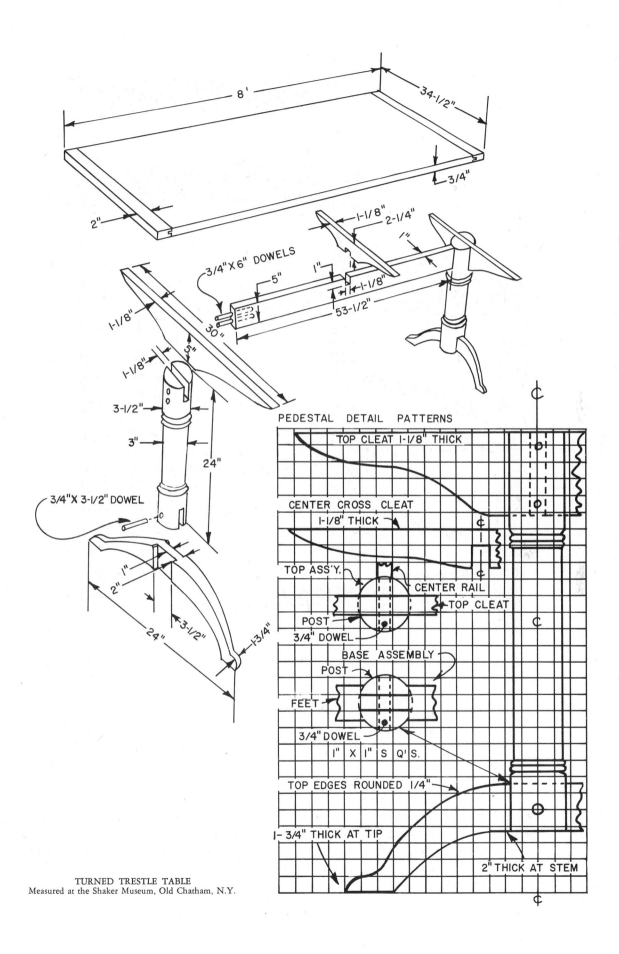

8'

34-1/2"

3/4"

2"

1-1/8" 2-1/4" 1"

3/4"X 6" DOWELS

1-1/8"

5"

1"

1-1/8"

53-1/2"

30"

1-1/8"

1-1/8"

5"

3-1/2"

3"

24"

3/4"X 3-1/2" DOWEL

1"

2"

3-1/2"

24"

1-3/4"

PEDESTAL DETAIL PATTERNS

TOP CLEAT 1-1/8" THICK

CENTER CROSS CLEAT

1-1/8" THICK

TOP ASS'Y.

CENTER RAIL

TOP CLEAT

POST

3/4" DOWEL

BASE ASSEMBLY

POST

FEET

3/4" DOWEL

1" X 1" SQ'S.

TOP EDGES ROUNDED 1/4"

1-3/4" THICK AT TIP

2" THICK AT STEM

₵

₵

₵

₵

₵

TURNED TRESTLE TABLE
Measured at the Shaker Museum, Old Chatham, N.Y.

149

DINING CHAIR

Two-slat dining chairs were designed to tuck under the tops of trestle tables. The earliest models were made with a single slat. The classical design shown above is believed to have been built by the Watervliet, New York, Shakers around 1830. The seat is woven with maple splints. This was used, along with hickory splints, on the very early chairs and rockers. *Photographed courtesy the Shaker Museum, Old Chatham, N.Y.*

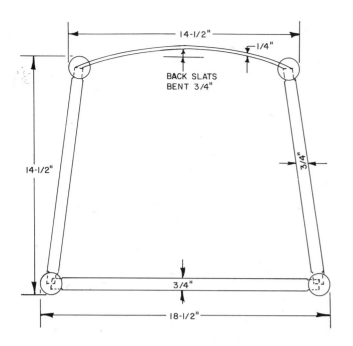

DINING CHAIR
Measured at the Shaker Museum, Old Chatham, N.Y.

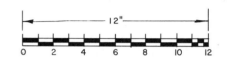

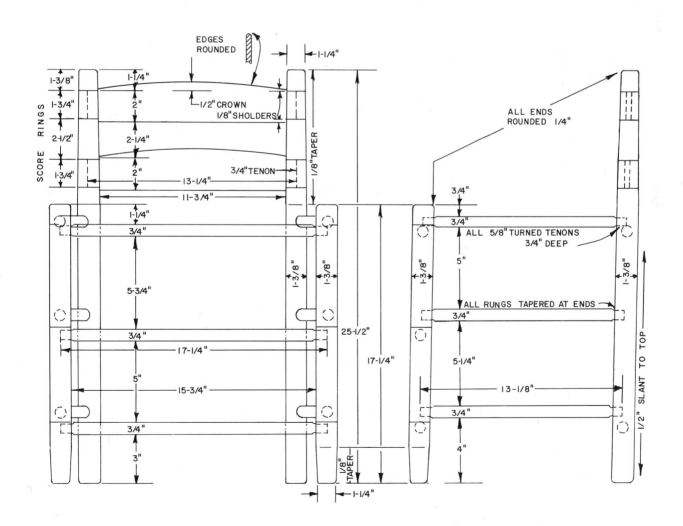

HARVARD TRESTLE TABLE

The functional attributes of Shaker design are aptly illustrated by this trestle table which was made at the Harvard community around 1840. The delicately curved standards and arched feet are joined with through mortises and tenons which were then pegged and braced for extra strength. The pine top is softened but not molded along the edges. This light but sturdy table is shorter than most Shaker trestles. This indicates it was probably designed for use by the Ministry. *Photographed courtesy Fruitlands Museums, Harvard, Mass.*

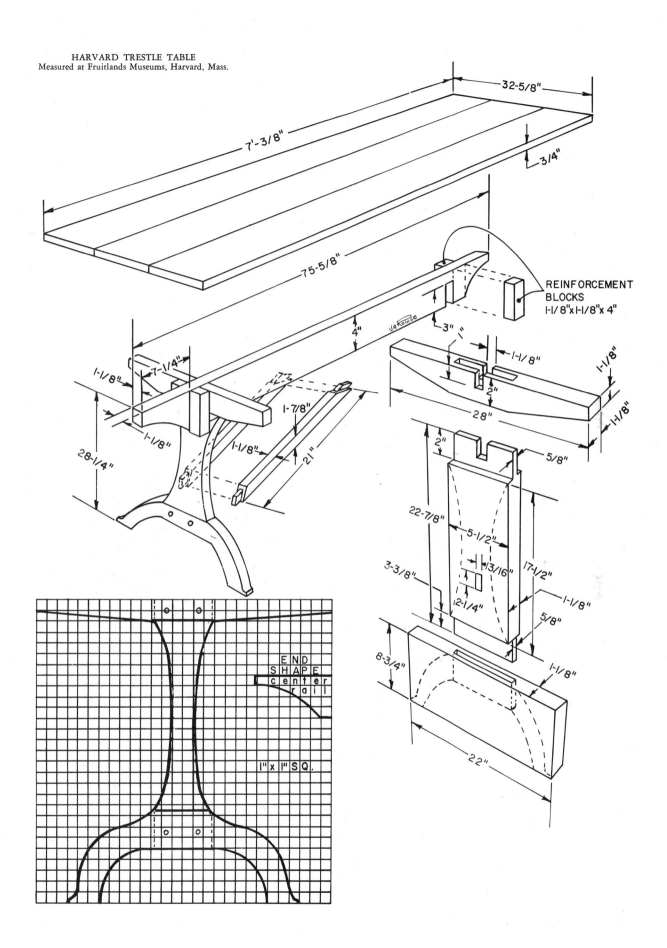

HARVARD TRESTLE TABLE
Measured at Fruitlands Museums, Harvard, Mass.

32-5/8"

7'-3/8"

3/4"

75-5/8"

REINFORCEMENT
BLOCKS
1-1/8"x 1-1/8"x 4"

4"

3"

1-1/8"

1-1/8"

1-1/8"

7-1/4"

1-1/8"

1-1/8"

1-7/8"

28"

2"

5/8"

1-1/8"

1-1/8"

2"

28-1/4"

21"

22-7/8"

5-1/2"

3/16"

17-1/2"

1-1/8"

3-3/8"

12-1/4"

5/8"

8-3/4"

1-1/8"

END
SHAPE
center
rail

1"x 1"SQ.

22"

MAPLE CHAIR

The art of chairmaking — at which the Shakers excelled — was brought to perfection in design and construction of the early ladder-back, illustrated above. Made at Harvard around the middle of the nineteenth century, this chair is exquisitely proportioned. The legs of curly maple are turned down and tapered to eliminate excess weight. Thin back slats of graduated widths are mildly bent to fit body contours. Unlike most chairs of this type, the seat is caned. Back legs are fitted with the Shakers' famous tilting attachment. *Photographed courtesy Fruitlands Museums, Harvard, Mass.*

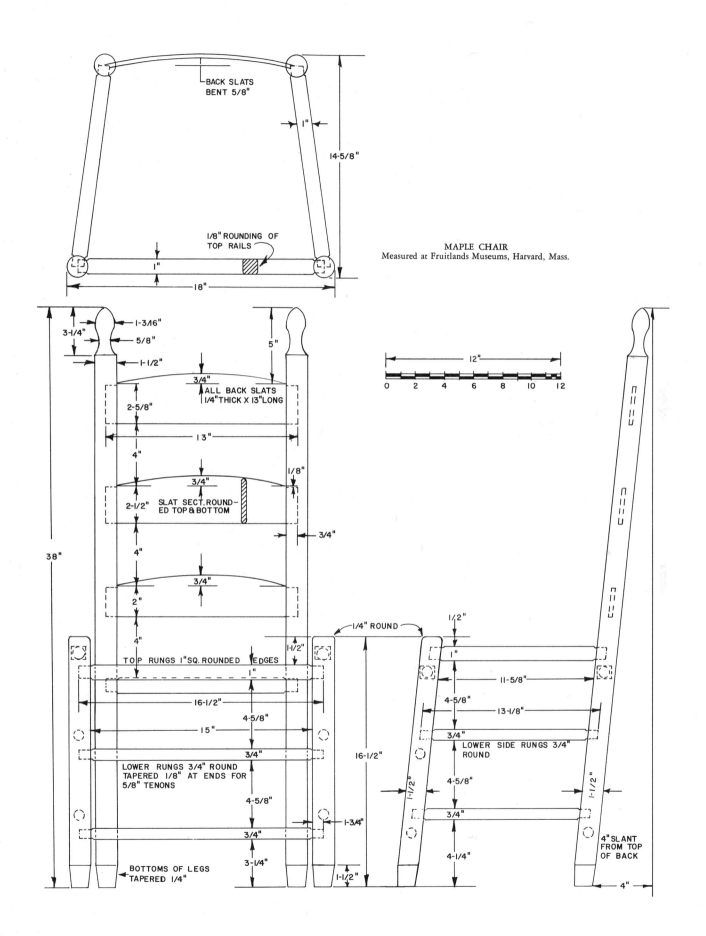

BACK SLATS
BENT 5/8"

1"

14-5/8"

1/8" ROUNDING OF
TOP RAILS

1"

18"

MAPLE CHAIR
Measured at Fruitlands Museums, Harvard, Mass.

1-3/16"
3-1/4"
5/8"
5"
1-1/2"

3/4"
ALL BACK SLATS
1/4"THICK X 13"LONG

2-5/8"

13"

4"

1/8"
3/4"

2-1/2"
SLAT SECT. ROUND-
ED TOP & BOTTOM

3/4"

4"

12"
0 2 4 6 8 10 12

3/4"

2"

4"

1/2"

1/4" ROUND

1-1/2"

38"

TOP RUNGS 1"SQ. ROUNDED EDGES

1"

1"

11-5/8"

16-1/2"

15"

4-5/8"

4-5/8"

13-1/8"

3/4"

3/4"

LOWER SIDE RUNGS 3/4"
ROUND

LOWER RUNGS 3/4" ROUND
TAPERED 1/8" AT ENDS FOR
5/8" TENONS

16-1/2"

1-1/2"

4-5/8"

4-5/8"

3/4"

3/4"

1-3/4"

4" SLANT
FROM TOP
OF BACK

BOTTOMS OF LEGS
TAPERED 1/4"

3-1/4"

1-1/2"

4-1/4"

1-1/2"

4"

155

SIDE TABLE

As a companion piece to the Harvard trestle table, shown on page 152, the little side table follows the same design and was probably made by the same Shaker craftsman. Like the larger table, it was built at Harvard around 1840. This lovely little table with its underslung drawer was probably designed to span a chair and thus facilitate sewing or other close work. *Photographed courtesy Fruitlands Museums, Harvard, Mass.*

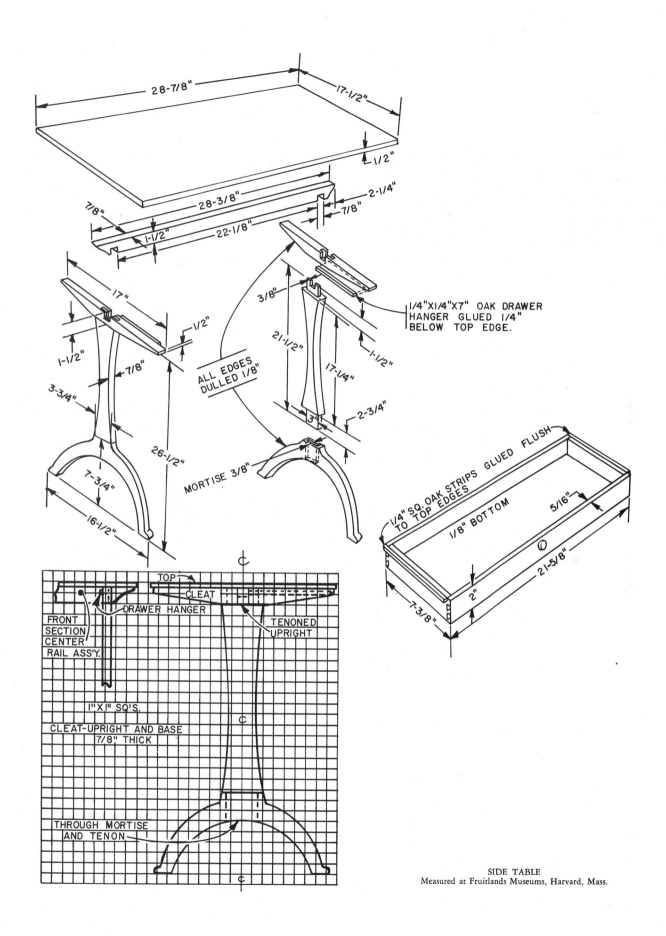

28-7/8"
17-1/2"
1/2"
28-3/8"
7/8"
2-1/4"
7/8"
1-1/2"
22-1/8"

17"
1/2"
3/8"
1/4"X1/4"X7" OAK DRAWER HANGER GLUED 1/4" BELOW TOP EDGE.
1-1/2"
7/8"
21-1/2"
17-1/4"
1-1/2"
3-3/4"
ALL EDGES DULLED 1/8"
26-1/2"
7-3/4"
MORTISE 3/8"
3"
2-3/4"
16-1/2"

1/4" SQ. OAK STRIPS GLUED FLUSH TO TOP EDGES
1/8" BOTTOM
5/16"
21-5/8"
2"
7-3/8"

TOP
CLEAT
DRAWER HANGER
FRONT SECTION CENTER RAIL ASS'Y.
TENONED UPRIGHT
1"X1" SQ'S.
CLEAT-UPRIGHT AND BASE 7/8" THICK
THROUGH MORTISE AND TENON

SIDE TABLE
Measured at Fruitlands Museums, Harvard, Mass.

157

DESK BOX

When traveling between communities, the Shaker elders and eldresses required specially designed boxes to carry their writing materials. Many of these were shaped as small, oblong chests, while others had slanted lids which served as writing counters. With its Queen Anne brass handles and bone key plate the one illustrated here, which was made at New Lebanon around 1870, is much more ornate than the earlier Shaker designs. *Photographed courtesy the Shaker Museum, Old Chatham, N.Y.*

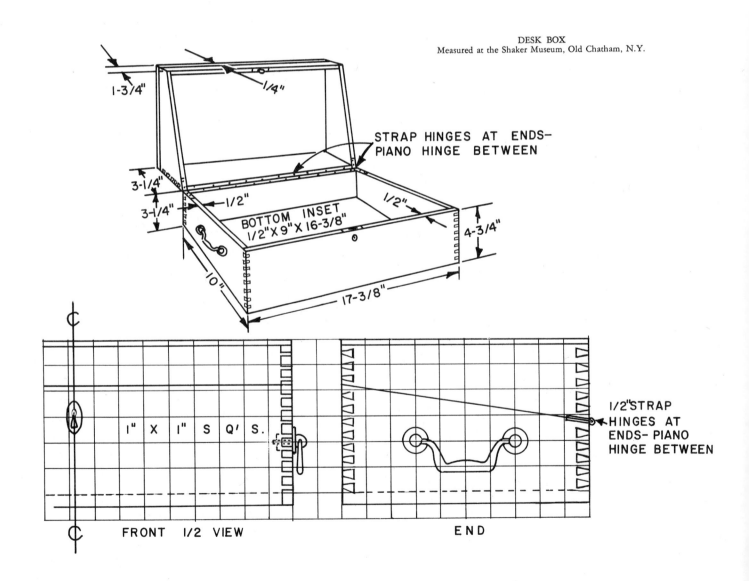

DESK BOX
Measured at the Shaker Museum, Old Chatham, N.Y.

1-3/4"

1/4"

STRAP HINGES AT ENDS—
PIANO HINGE BETWEEN

3-1/4"

1/2"

1/2"

3-1/4"

BOTTOM INSET
1/2" X 9" X 16-3/8"

4-3/4"

10"

17-3/8"

1" X 1" SQ'S.

1/2" STRAP HINGES AT ENDS— PIANO HINGE BETWEEN

FRONT 1/2 VIEW

END

LAP DESK

The slant-lid lap desk, which was made at New Lebanon around 1850, is believed to have been used by Eldress Emma Neale. Made of maple, this design is notable for its flawless craftsmanship. The intricate dovetailing of parts and fitting of the little drawer exemplifies the precise skill applied by the Shakers to the construction of even their simplest objects. *Photographed courtesy the Shaker Museum, Old Chatham, N.Y.*

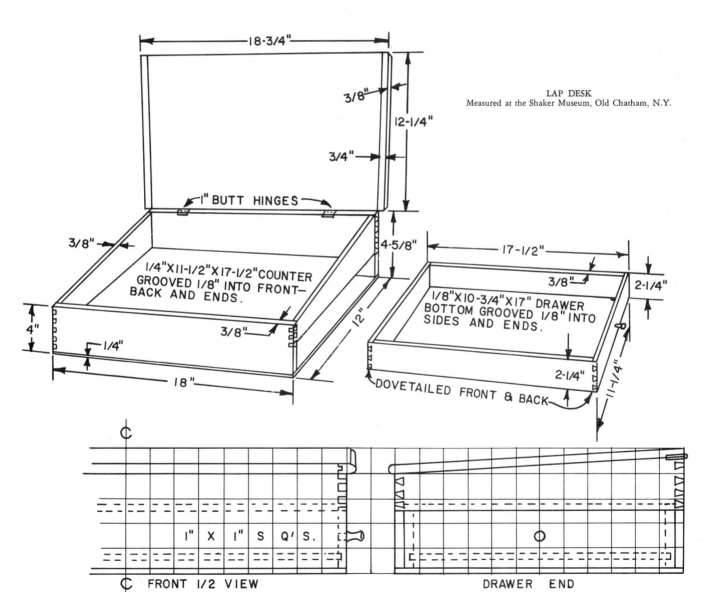

LAP DESK
Measured at the Shaker Museum, Old Chatham, N.Y.

18-3/4"

3/8"

12-1/4"

3/4"

1" BUTT HINGES

3/8"

4-5/8"

1/4"X11-1/2"X17-1/2"COUNTER GROOVED 1/8" INTO FRONT-BACK AND ENDS.

4"

12"

1/4"

3/8"

18"

17-1/2"

3/8"

2-1/4"

1/8"X10-3/4"X17" DRAWER BOTTOM GROOVED 1/8" INTO SIDES AND ENDS.

2-1/4"

11-1/4"

DOVETAILED FRONT & BACK

1" X 1" S Q'S.

FRONT 1/2 VIEW

DRAWER END

159

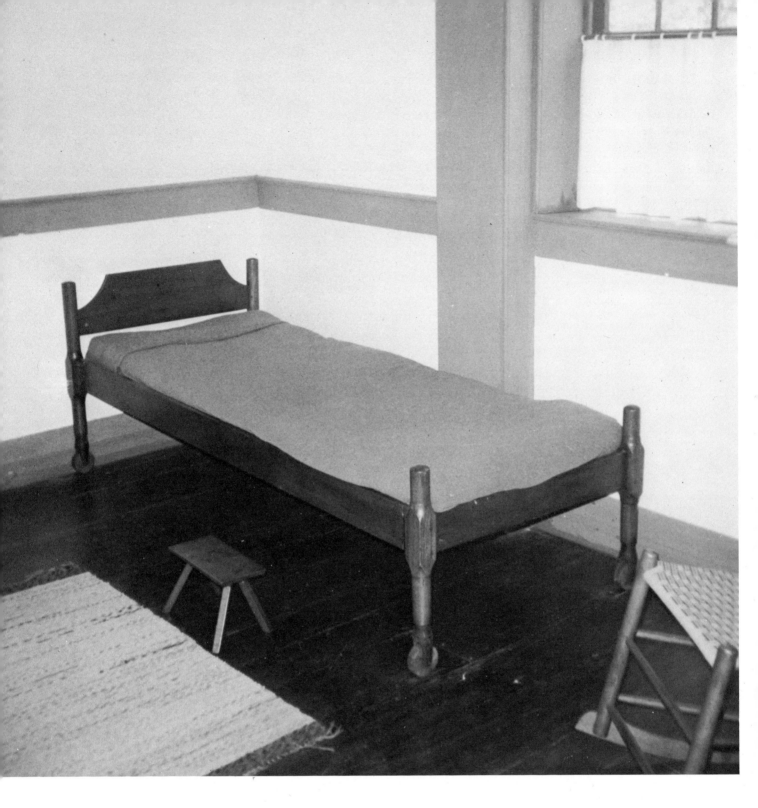

BED

Shaker beds were plain and practical. But like all things Shaker, they had their own independent style. The maple bed shown here is typical. This one was built at Hancock around 1830. It was mounted on wooden rollers, which enabled the Shaker Sisters to draw it away from the wall during the daily bedmaking routine. The slim mattress, filled with corn husks or feathers, was suspended on rope webbing. *Photographed courtesy Hancock Shaker Village, Hancock, Mass.*

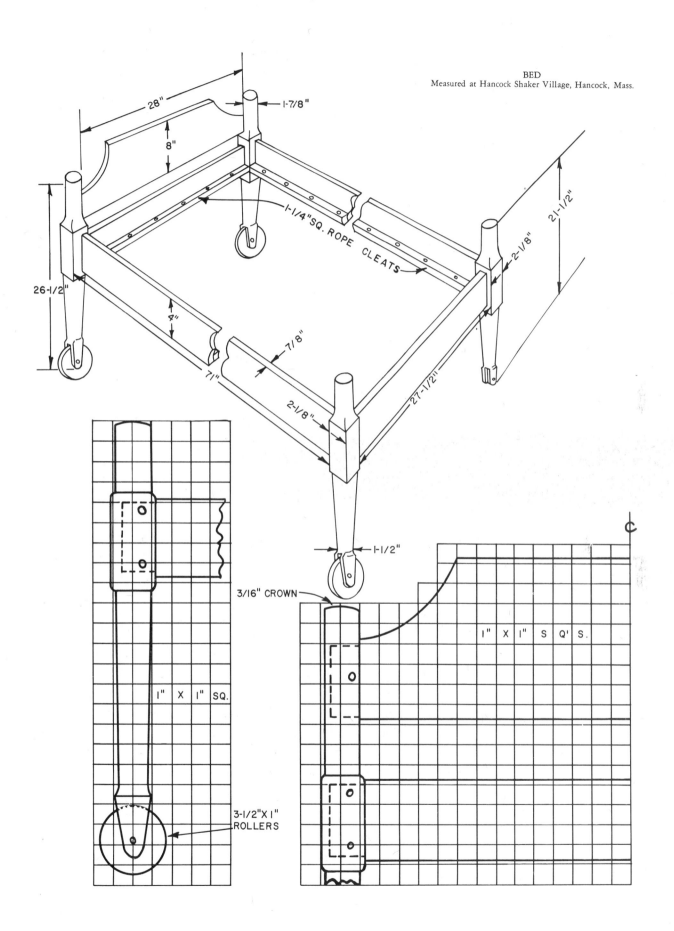

BED
Measured at Hancock Shaker Village, Hancock, Mass.

28"

1-7/8"

8"

26-1/2"

1-1/4" SQ. ROPE CLEATS

21-1/2"

2-1/8"

4"

7/8"

71"

2-1/8"

27-1/2"

1-1/2"

3/16" CROWN

1" X 1" SQ'S.

1" X 1" SQ.

3-1/2" X 1"
ROLLERS

161

SETTEE

This classic of Shaker design is believed to have originated at Canterbury, New Hampshire, around 1830. It was copied and made in varying lengths at several other Shaker communities. Usually the seats were shaped of pine, with the back spindles and legs turned of maple. *Photographed courtesy the Shaker Museum, Old Chatham, N.Y.*

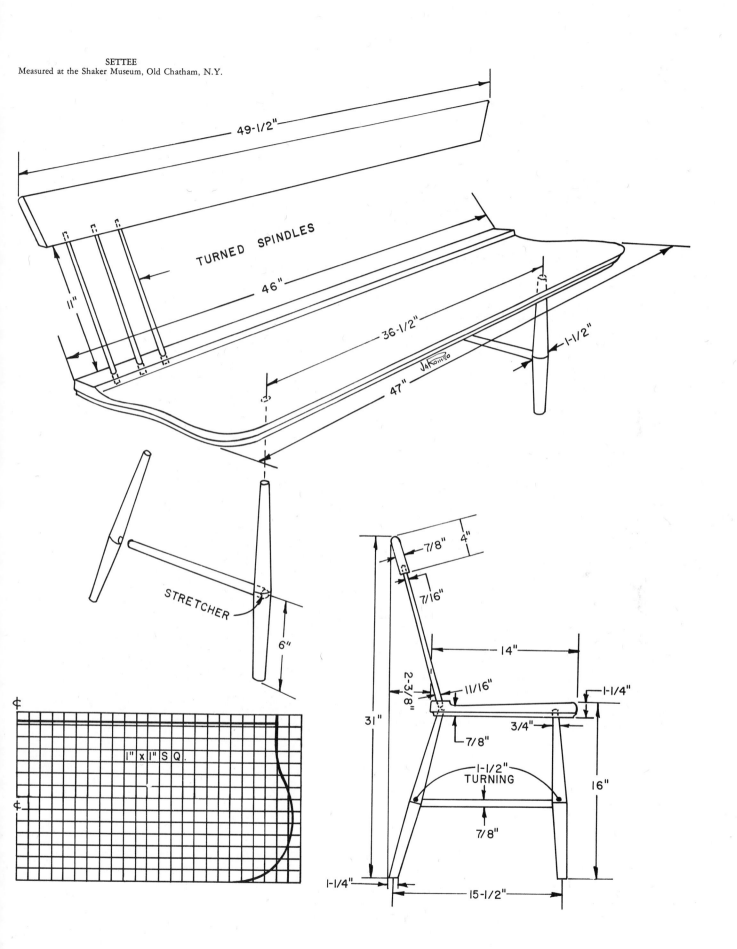

SETTEE
Measured at the Shaker Museum, Old Chatham, N.Y.

49-1/2"

TURNED SPINDLES

11"

46"

36-1/2"

1-1/2"

47"

STRETCHER

6"

1" x 1" SQ.

7/8"   4"

7/16"

14"

2-3/8"

11/16"

1-1/4"

3/4"

31"

7/8"

1-1/2"
TURNING

16"

7/8"

1-1/4"

15-1/2"

163

NIGHT STAND

Shaker craftsmen often retained good designs over unlimited periods of time. The little pine night stand shown here was built at Hancock in 1875, but the basic design may have originated fifty years earlier. All details of its construction tend to identify it with pieces made much earlier in the nineteenth century. *Photographed courtesy the Shaker Museum, Sabbathday Lake, Maine.*

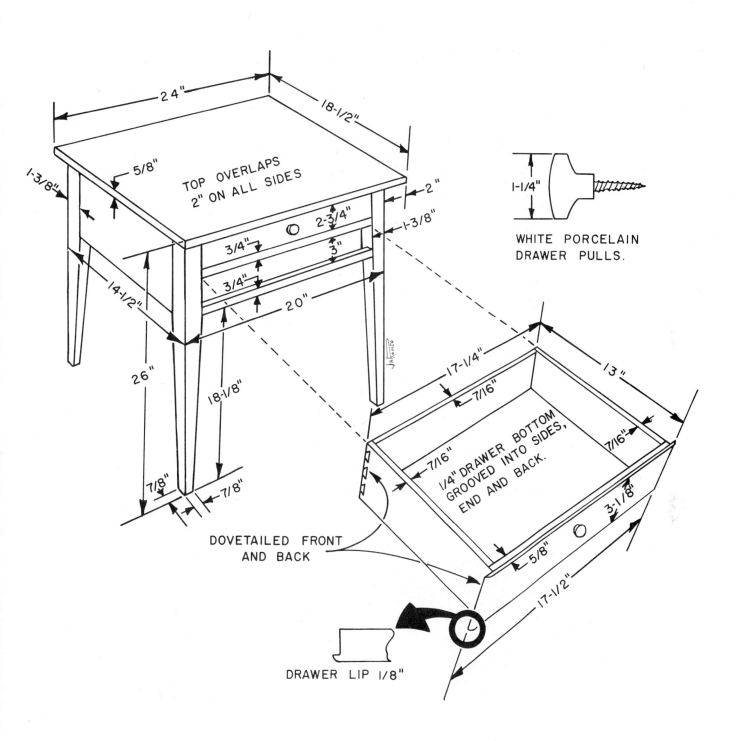

24"

18-1/2"

5/8"

1-3/8"

TOP OVERLAPS
2" ON ALL SIDES

2"

1-3/8"

2-3/4"

3/4"

3"

3/4"

14-1/2"

20"

26"

18-1/8"

7/8"

7/8"

1-1/4"

WHITE PORCELAIN
DRAWER PULLS.

17-1/4"

13"

7/16"

7/16"

7/16"

1/4" DRAWER BOTTOM
GROOVED INTO SIDES,
END AND BACK.

3-1/8"

5/8"

17-1/2"

DOVETAILED FRONT
AND BACK

DRAWER LIP 1/8"

NIGHT STAND
Measured at the Shaker Museum, Sabbathday Lake, Me.

165

HIGH CHAIR

This high chair, which was built at Union Village, Ohio, early in the nineteenth century, apparently was not designed for children. Its size and sturdiness of construction suggests it may have been used as an ironing chair, or for other adult work which required an elevated seating position. *Photographed courtesy the Golden Lamb Inn, Lebanon, O.*

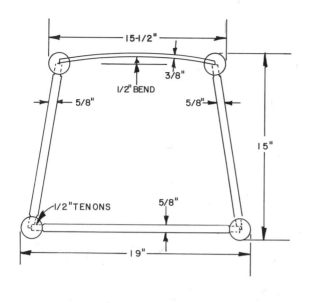

15-1/2"

3/8"

1/2" BEND

5/8"   5/8"

15"

1/2" TENONS   5/8"

19"

HIGH CHAIR
Measured at the Golden Lamb Inn, Lebanon, O.

12"

0 2 4 6 8 10 12

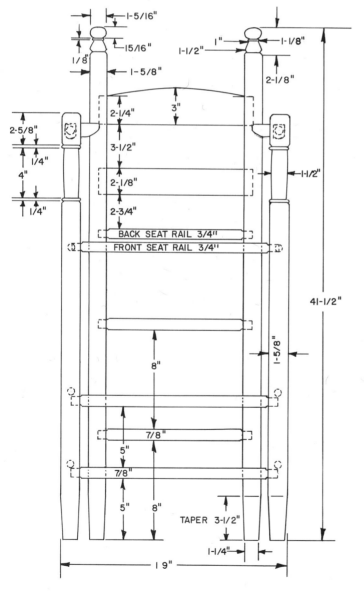

1-5/16"

15/16"

1/8"

1-5/8"

1-1/2"   1"

1-1/8"

2-1/8"

2-5/8"

1/4"

4"

1/4"

3"

2-1/4"

3-1/2"

2-1/8"

2-3/4"

BACK SEAT RAIL 3/4"

FRONT SEAT RAIL 3/4"

1-1/2"

41-1/2"

1-5/8"

8"

7/8"

5"

5"   8"

7/8"

TAPER 3-1/2"

1-1/4"

19"

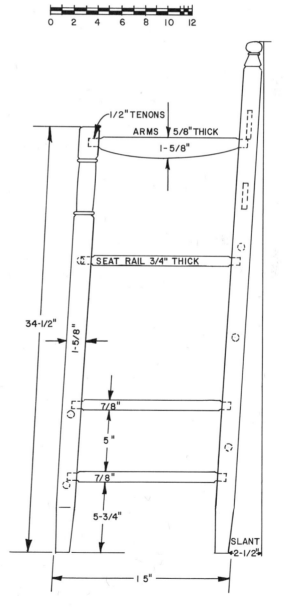

1/2" TENONS

ARMS   5/8" THICK

1-5/8"

SEAT RAIL 3/4" THICK

34-1/2"

1-5/8"

7/8"

5"

7/8"

5-3/4"

SLANT
2-1/2"

15"

167

BLANKET CHEST

The Shakers of New Lebanon or Watervliet, New York, where this chest was built around 1820, simply called it a "blanket box." It was made of pumpkin pine, carefully dovetailed at all corners. This was the fundamental structure in progression of the Shakers' lidded chests. In later designs, they were elevated to contain one, two, or three drawers while still retaining the lidded top compartment. *Photographed by Lees Studio courtesy the Shaker Museum, Old Chatham, N.Y.*

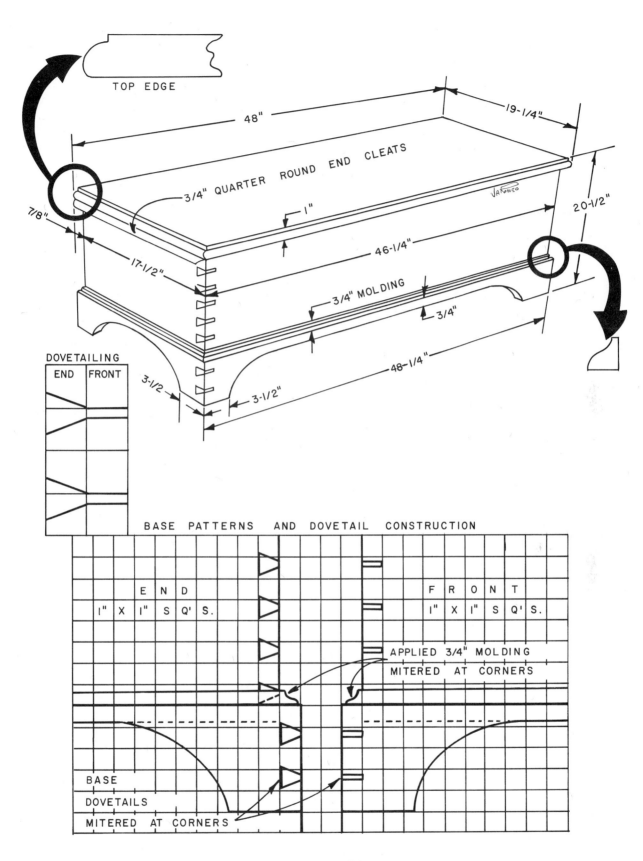

TOP EDGE

48"

19-1/4"

3/4" QUARTER ROUND END CLEATS

1"

7/8"

20-1/2"

17-1/2"

46-1/4"

3/4" MOLDING

3/4"

3-1/2"

48-1/4"

3-1/2"

DOVETAILING

END | FRONT

BASE PATTERNS AND DOVETAIL CONSTRUCTION

E N D

1" X 1" SQ'S.

F R O N T

1" X 1" SQ'S.

APPLIED 3/4" MOLDING

MITERED AT CORNERS

BASE

DOVETAILS

MITERED AT CORNERS

BLANKET CHEST
Measured at the Shaker Museum, Old Chatham, N.Y.

DROP-LEAF TABLE

The Shakers would abhor use of the term "elegant" in reference to any of their work. But in its perfect proportioning of parts and fine details of craftsmanship, this cherry table, which was made at Hancock around 1830, is indeed an elegant piece of furniture. *Photographed by Lees Studio courtesy the Shaker Museum, Old Chatham, N.Y.*

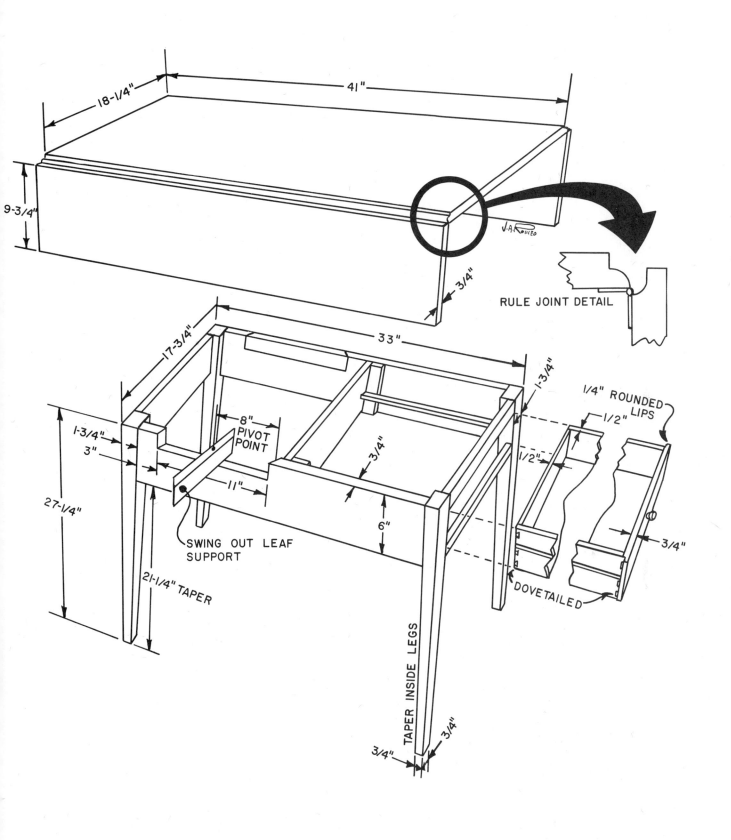

18-1/4"

41"

9-3/4"

3/4"

RULE JOINT DETAIL

17-3/4"

33"

1-3/4"

1/4" ROUNDED LIPS

1/2"

1-3/4"

1/2"

3"

8"
PIVOT
POINT

3/4"

27-1/4"

11"

6"

3/4"

SWING OUT LEAF
SUPPORT

21-1/4" TAPER

DOVETAILED

TAPER INSIDE LEGS

3/4"

3/4"

3/4"

DROP-LEAF TABLE
Measured at the Shaker Museum, Old Chatham, N.Y.

171

SEWING CHEST

Built by the Shakers of Enfield, Connecticut, around 1830, this chest of pumpkin pine is another one-and-only which apparently was custom-designed to meet the needs of certain individuals. The drawers could be pulled out from opposite ends, making it possible for two people to work across from each other with mutual access to the large front drawer. *Photographed by Lees Studio courtesy the Shaker Museum, Old Chatham, N.Y.*

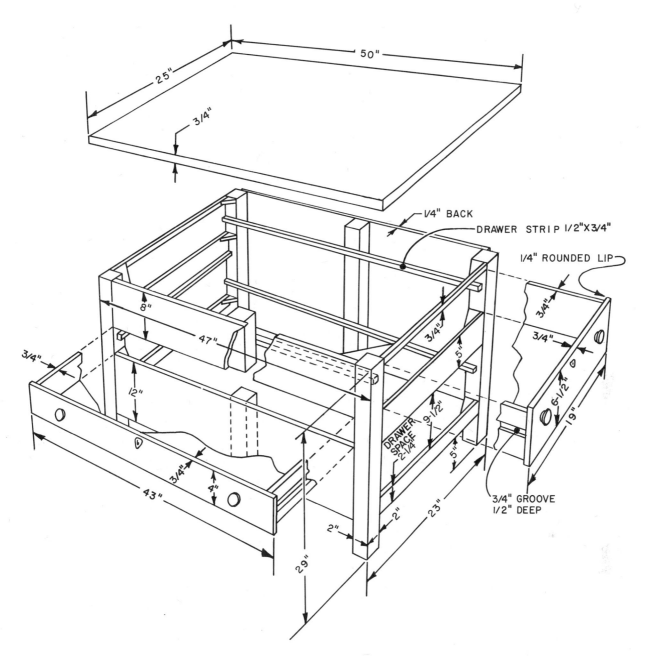

50"

25"

3/4"

1/4" BACK

DRAWER STRIP 1/2"X3/4"

1/4" ROUNDED LIP

3/4"

3/4"

8"

47"

3/4"

3/4"

6-1/2"

19"

12"

3/4"

4"

43"

DRAWER SPACE 2-1/4"

9-1/2"

5"

5"

3/4" GROOVE 1/2" DEEP

2"

2"

23"

29"

SEWING CHEST
Measured at the Shaker Museum, Old Chatham, N.Y.

173

STRETCHER TABLE

Shakers often mixed their woods in construction of a single article. This trim stretcher table, which was built at New Lebanon around 1830, used cherry for the top, skirts, and drawer front and birch for the turned legs and stretchers. *Photographed courtesy Hancock Shaker Village, Hancock, Mass.*

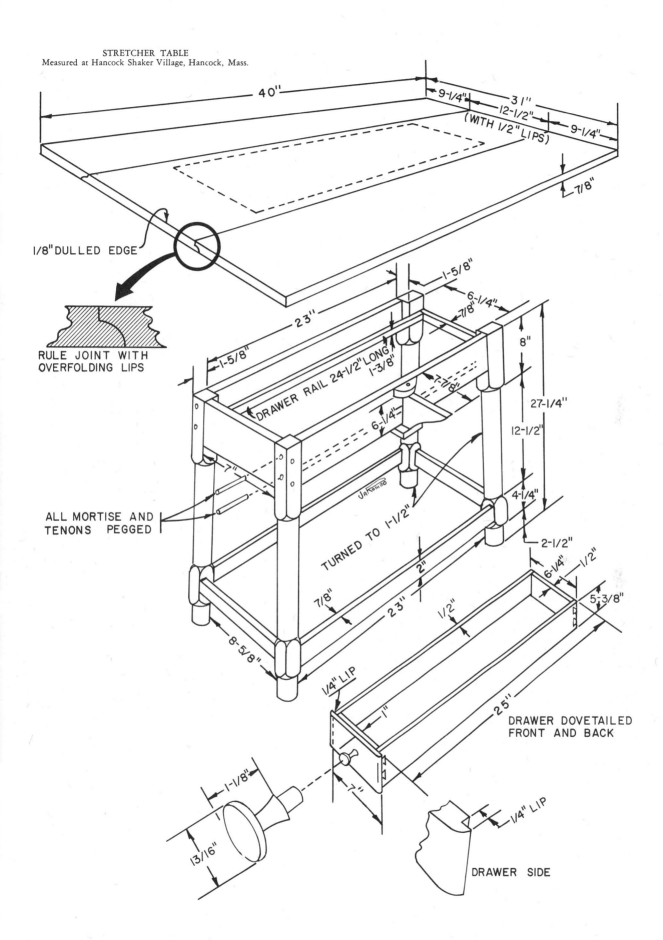

STRETCHER TABLE
Measured at Hancock Shaker Village, Hancock, Mass.

40"

9-1/4"   31"
12-1/2"
(WITH 1/2" LIPS)   9-1/4"

7/8"

1/8" DULLED EDGE

RULE JOINT WITH
OVERFOLDING LIPS

1-5/8"
6-1/4"
7/8"
8"

23"

1-5/8"
DRAWER RAIL 24-1/2" LONG
1-3/8"

27-1/4"

6-1/4"
12-1/2"

ALL MORTISE AND
TENONS PEGGED

7"

4-1/4"

2-1/2"

TURNED TO 1-1/2"
2"

6-1/4"   1/2"

7/8"   23"   1/2"   5-3/8"

8-5/8"

25"

1/4" LIP
1"
DRAWER DOVETAILED
FRONT AND BACK

1-1/8"

7"

13/16"

1/4" LIP

DRAWER SIDE

175

LIDDED CHEST WITH ONE DRAWER

This chest with a single drawer was built at Harvard or Shirley, Massachusetts, circa 1840. The design indicates how the plain box-type chest, without drawers, evolved with elevation, and addition of drawers at the bottom, into a full chest of drawers. Oddly, the Shakers retained the lidded tops for more than a century after early American craftsmen had discarded them. *Photographed courtesy Fruitlands Museums, Harvard, Mass.*

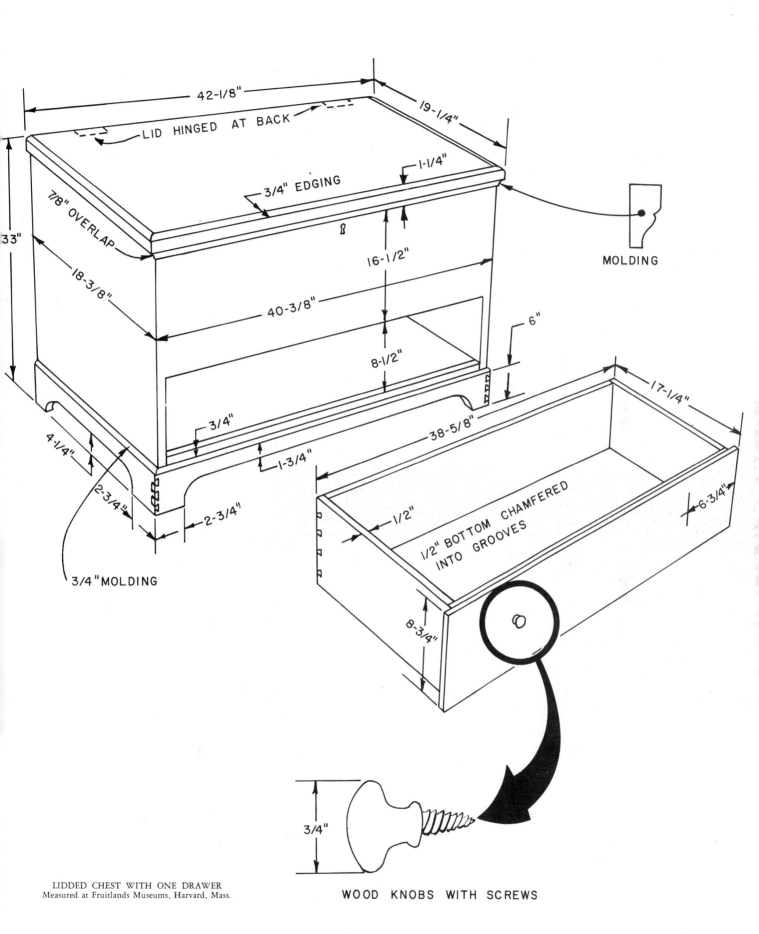

42-1/8"

LID HINGED AT BACK

19-1/4"

3/4" EDGING

1-1/4"

7/8" OVERLAP

33"

16-1/2"

MOLDING

18-3/8"

40-3/8"

6"

8-1/2"

17-1/4"

3/4"

38-5/8"

4-1/4"

1-3/4"

6-3/4"

2-3/4"

1/2"

2-3/4"

1/2" BOTTOM CHAMFERED
INTO GROOVES

3/4" MOLDING

8-3/4"

3/4"

LIDDED CHEST WITH ONE DRAWER
Measured at Fruitlands Museums, Harvard, Mass.

WOOD KNOBS WITH SCREWS

CHILD'S DESK

Children placed in the Shakers' care were attentively schooled to the standards of local and state educational laws. Rarely, however, did they enjoy the use of desks as nicely constructed as this pine model, which was built at Watervliet, New York, around 1880. *Photographed courtesy the Shaker Museum, Old Chatham, N.Y.*

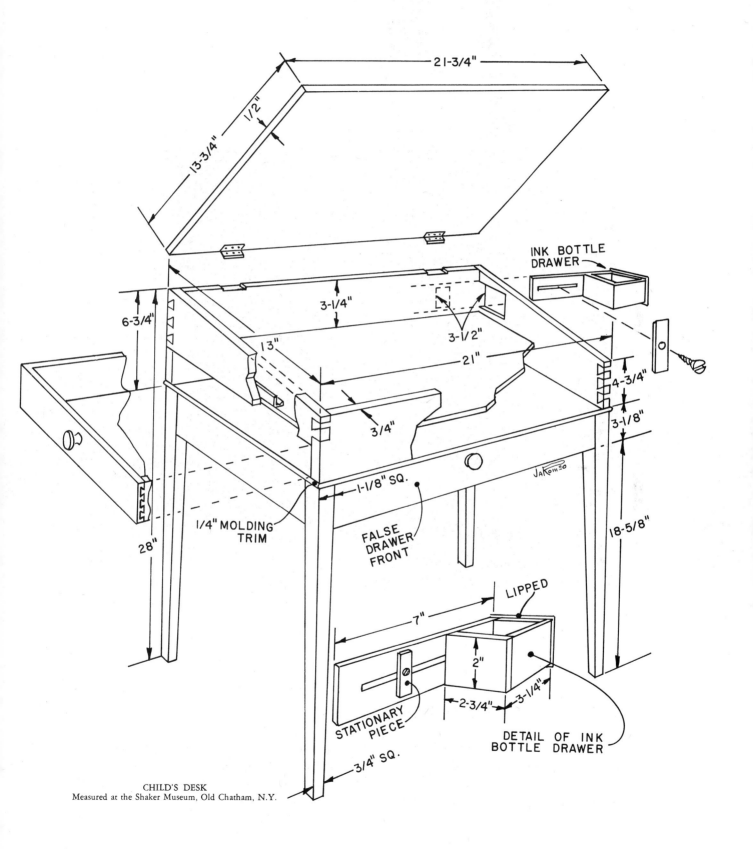

21-3/4"

1/2"

13-3/4"

INK BOTTLE
DRAWER

6-3/4"

3-1/4"

3-1/2"

13"

21"

4-3/4"

3/4"

3-1/8"

1/4" MOLDING
TRIM

1-1/8" SQ.

FALSE
DRAWER
FRONT

18-5/8"

28"

LIPPED

7"

2"

STATIONARY
PIECE

2-3/4"   3-1/4"

DETAIL OF INK
BOTTLE DRAWER

3/4" SQ.

CHILD'S DESK
Measured at the Shaker Museum, Old Chatham, N.Y.

JaRomzo

179

LIDDED CHEST WITH TWO DRAWERS

With addition of bottom drawers, the box-type chest evolved into a full chest of drawers. But as this design indicates, it could be a rather handsome piece of furniture even before the ultimate development was accomplished. This lidded chest of pumpkin pine was built at New Lebanon around 1820. *Photographed courtesy the Shaker Museum, Old Chatham, N.Y.*

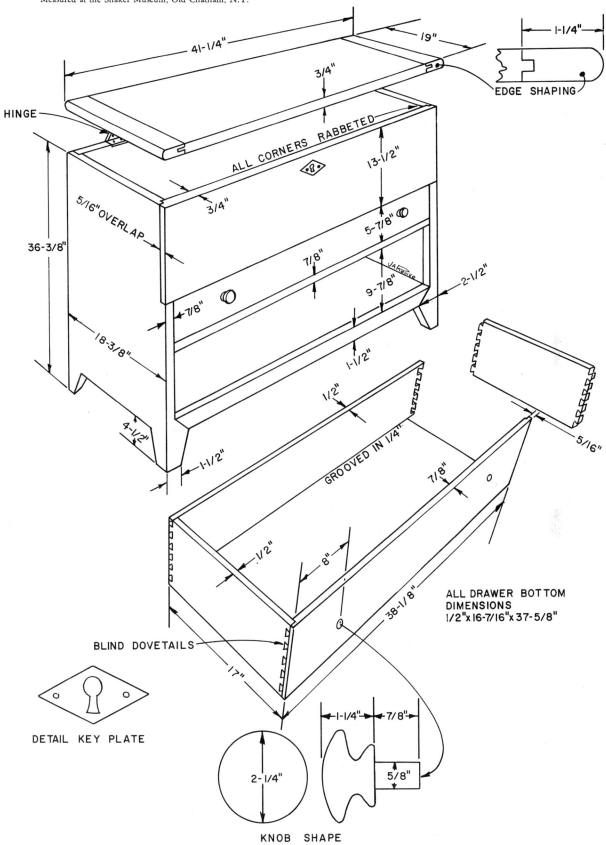

LIDDED CHEST WITH TWO DRAWERS
Measured at the Shaker Museum, Old Chatham, N.Y.

41-1/4"

19"

1-1/4"

3/4"

EDGE SHAPING

HINGE

ALL CORNERS RABBETED

13-1/2"

3/4"

5/16" OVERLAP

3/4"

5-7/8"

36-3/8"

7/8"

9-7/8"

2-1/2"

7/8"

18-3/8"

1-1/2"

1/2"

1-1/2"

4-1/2"

GROOVED IN 1/4"

7/8"

5/16"

1/2"

8"

ALL DRAWER BOTTOM
DIMENSIONS
1/2"x16-7/16"x37-5/8"

BLIND DOVETAILS

38-1/8"

17"

DETAIL KEY PLATE

1-1/4"   7/8"

5/8"

2-1/4"

KNOB SHAPE

181

PEDESTAL TABLES

Another area in which the Shakers carried their craftsmanship to a point of artistic perfection was in the design and construction of pedestal tables. Most Shaker pedestals are beautifully proportioned and balanced. The best examples have tapered or symmetrically turned stems which are dovetailed to undulating or gracefully arched legs.

The maple pedestal on this page was made at New Lebanon around 1830. Top tenon of the original model was threaded into the disk plate, which, in turn, was screw-fastened to the top.

PEDESTAL TABLE
Measured at the Shaker Museum, Old Chatham, N.Y.

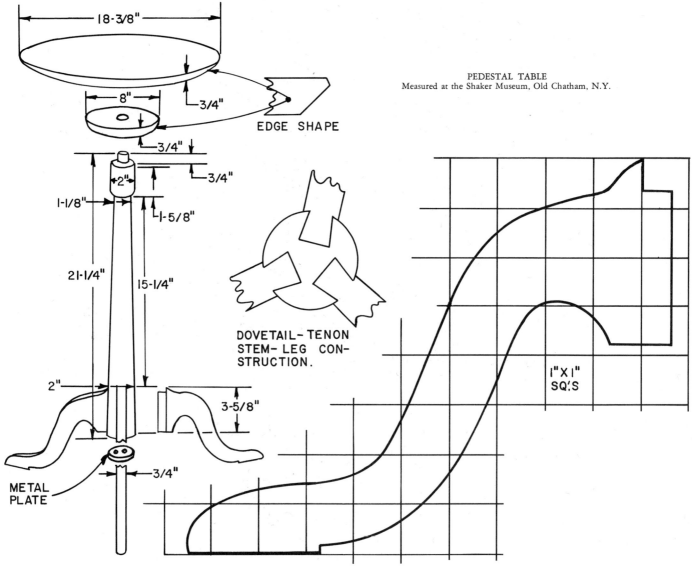

18-3/8"

8"

3/4"

EDGE SHAPE

3/4"

3/4"

2"

1-1/8"

1-5/8"

21-1/4"

15-1/4"

DOVETAIL-TENON STEM-LEG CONSTRUCTION.

2"

3-5/8"

1"X1" SQ'S

METAL PLATE

3/4"

Perhaps the most beautiful pedestal table ever built by the Shakers was the cherry design on this page. The original table, shown here, was made at Hancock around 1830. Copies were made at other communities, and the design is now widely reproduced. But there is significant subtlety to the turning of the stem which joins with the tapered, arched legs to form a design composition of exquisite harmony. This is seldom captured in reproductions of the design, which are usually distorted with bulbous stems and misshapen legs. *Table on page 182 photographed courtesy the Shaker Museum, Old Chatham, N.Y.; table on page 183 photographed courtesy Hancock Shaker Village, Hancock, Mass.*

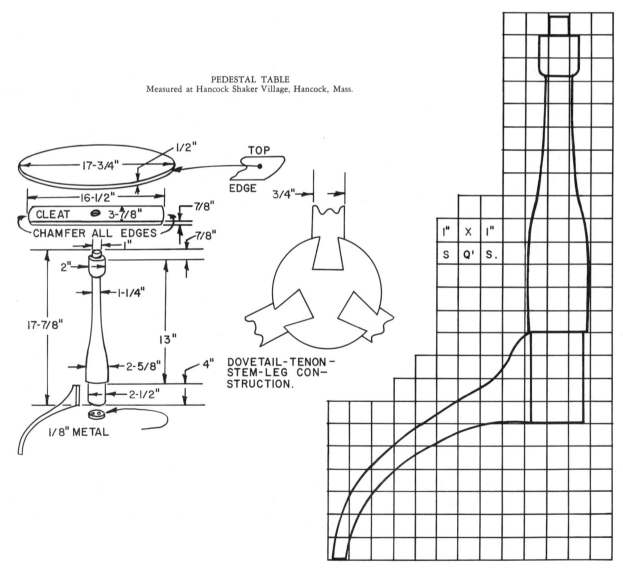

PEDESTAL TABLE
Measured at Hancock Shaker Village, Hancock, Mass.

LIDDED CHEST WITH THREE DRAWERS

The pine chest built at Enfield, New Hampshire, during the mid-nineteenth century was among the last of the Shaker lidded chests. Most case pieces made then, and thereafter, were designed as full chests of drawers — with a top drawer replacing the lidded compartment. However, since this was used as a blanket chest there was definite advantage to having the top lidded for easy access. *Photographed courtesy the Shaker Museum, Sabbathday Lake, Me.*

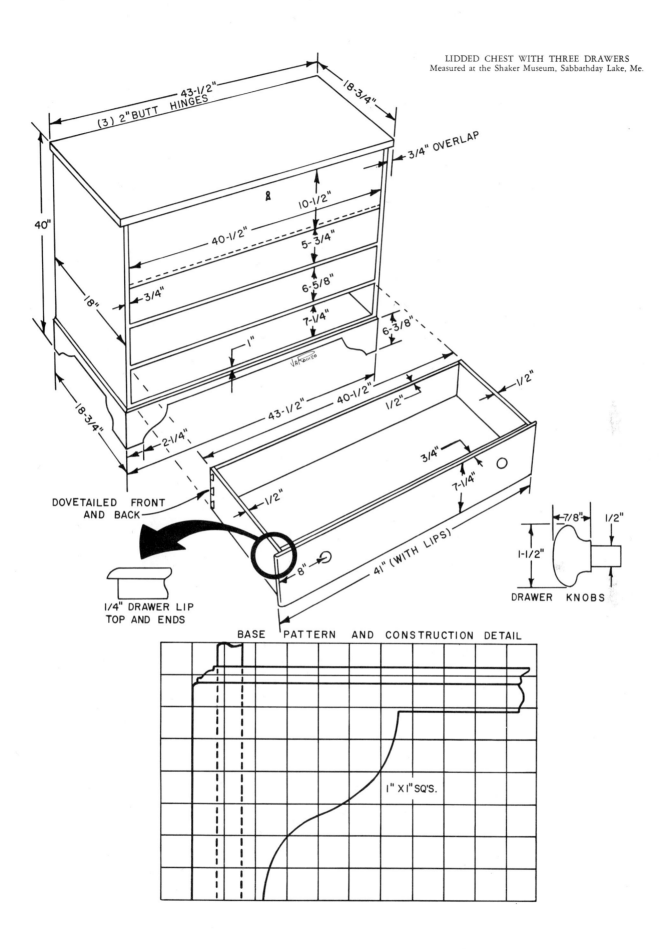

43-1/2"

(3) 2" BUTT HINGES

18-3/4"

3/4" OVERLAP

10-1/2"

40"

40-1/2"

5-3/4"

18"

6-5/8"

3/4"

7-1/4"

6-3/8"

1"

18-3/4"

2-1/4"

43-1/2"   40-1/2"   1/2"

1/2"

3/4"

7-1/4"

7/8"   1/2"

1-1/2"

DRAWER KNOBS

DOVETAILED FRONT
AND BACK

1/2"

8"

41" (WITH LIPS)

1/4" DRAWER LIP
TOP AND ENDS

BASE PATTERN AND CONSTRUCTION DETAIL

1" X 1" SQ'S.

185

SEWING DESK

Among the oldest of the Shaker sewing desks is the design shown above. This was built at Sabbathday Lake, Maine, around 1815. It is made of pine which has been stained a reddish-orange tone. *Photographed courtesy the Shaker Museum, Sabbathday Lake, Me.*

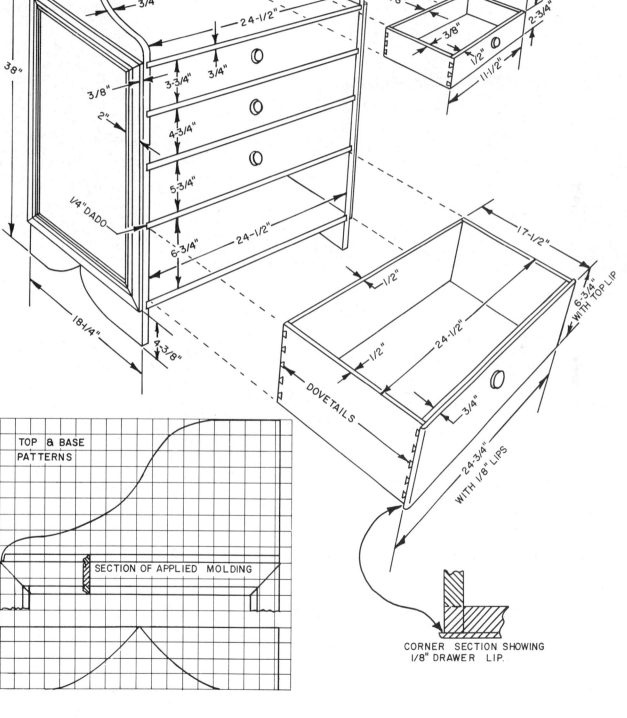

SECTION
1/2 ROUNDED
EDGES

26"
3/4"
5"
2-1/2"
1/2"
9"
2-3/4"
1/2"
1/2"
3/4"
24-1/2"

5"
3/8"
2-3/4"
3/8"
1/2"
11-1/2"

3/8"
2"
3-3/4"
3/4"
4-3/4"
38"
5-3/4"
1/4" DADO
6-3/4"
24-1/2"
18-1/4"
4-3/8"

17-1/2"
1/2"
6-3/4"
WITH TOP LIP
1/2"
24-1/2"
DOVETAILS
3/4"
24-3/4"
WITH 1/8" LIPS

TOP & BASE
PATTERNS

SECTION OF APPLIED MOLDING

CORNER SECTION SHOWING
1/8" DRAWER LIP.

187

ROCKING CHAIR

This handsome rocker was made by the Wagan Company of Shaker craftsmen, at Mt. (New) Lebanon, New York, sometime after 1860. It displays the fine details of construction and harmony of proportions which made Shaker rocking chairs so appealing. Worsted tape, used for weaving the back and seat, came in bright colors and was often woven in contrasting, checkerboard patterns. The rockers were finished in natural stain and varnish or in lustrous ebony. *Photographed courtesy Hancock Shaker Village, Hancock, Mass.*

ROCKING CHAIR
Measured at Hancock Shaker Village, Hancock, Mass.

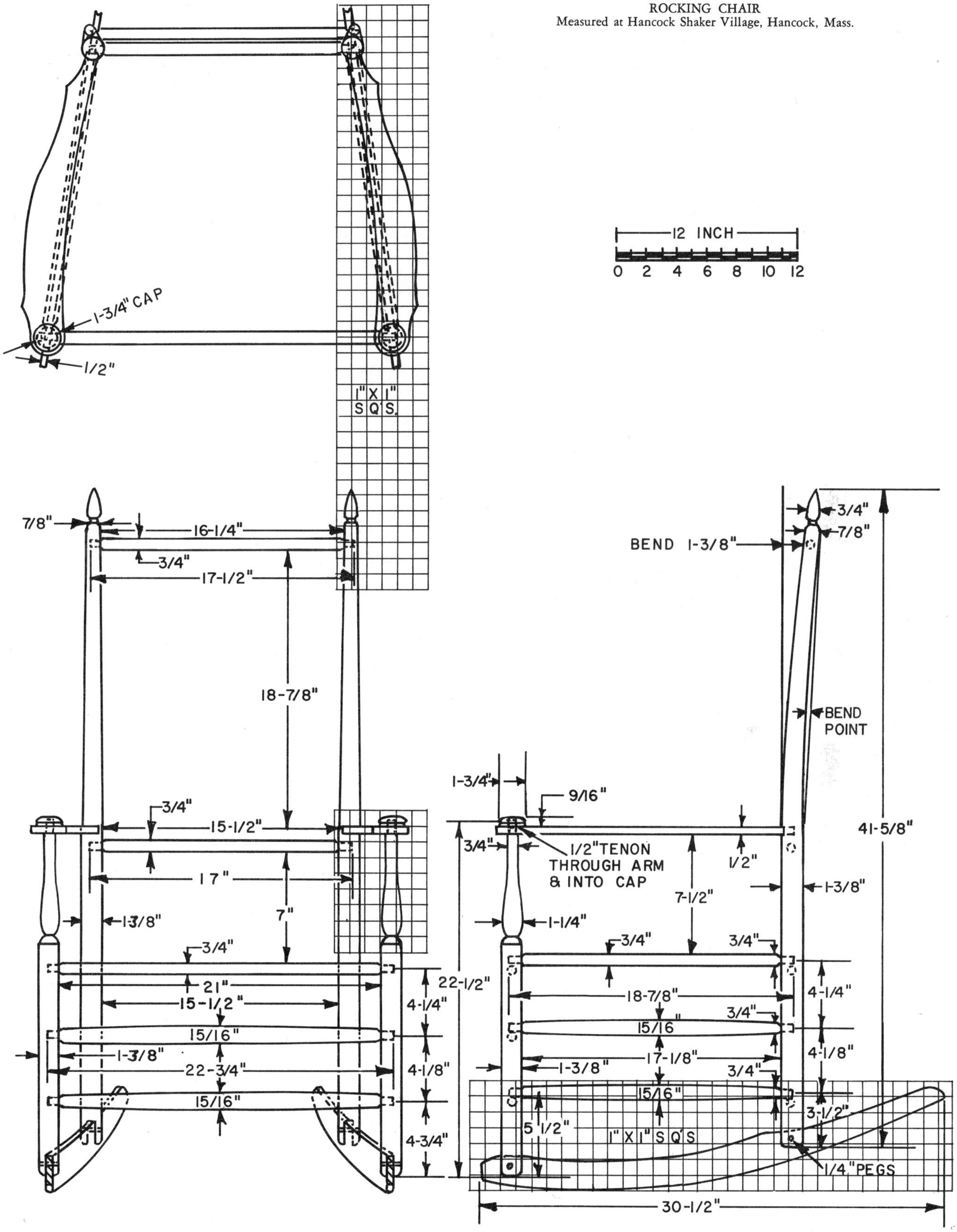

12 INCH
0 2 4 6 8 10 12

1-3/4" CAP
1/2"

1" X 1" SQS.

7/8"
16-1/4"
3/4"
17-1/2"

18-7/8"

3/4"
15-1/2"
17"
7"
1-3/8"
3/4"
21"
15-1/2"
15/16"
1-3/8"
22-3/4"
15/16"
22-1/2"
4-1/4"
4-1/8"
4-3/4"

BEND 1-3/8"
3/4"
7/8"

BEND POINT

41-5/8"

1-3/4"
9/16"
3/4"
1/2" TENON THROUGH ARM & INTO CAP
7-1/2"
1/2"
1-3/8"
1-1/4"
3/4"
3/4"
18-7/8"
3/4"
15/16"
1-3/8"
17-1/8"
3/4"
15/16"
5 1/2"
1" X 1" SQS
4-1/4"
4-1/8"
3-1/2"
1/4" PEGS
30-1/2"

189

MAPLE TABLE

The one way in which Shaker craftsmen would tolerate decoration of their work was in the selection of beautifully grained woods. The curly and birds-eye maple used in construction of this table was obviously selected with considerable care. Thus the natural grain patterns of the top, legs, and aprons are perfectly matched. This maple table is believed to have been made at Canterbury, New Hampshire, in the mid-nineteenth century. *Photographed courtesy the Shaker Museum, Old Chatham, N.Y.*

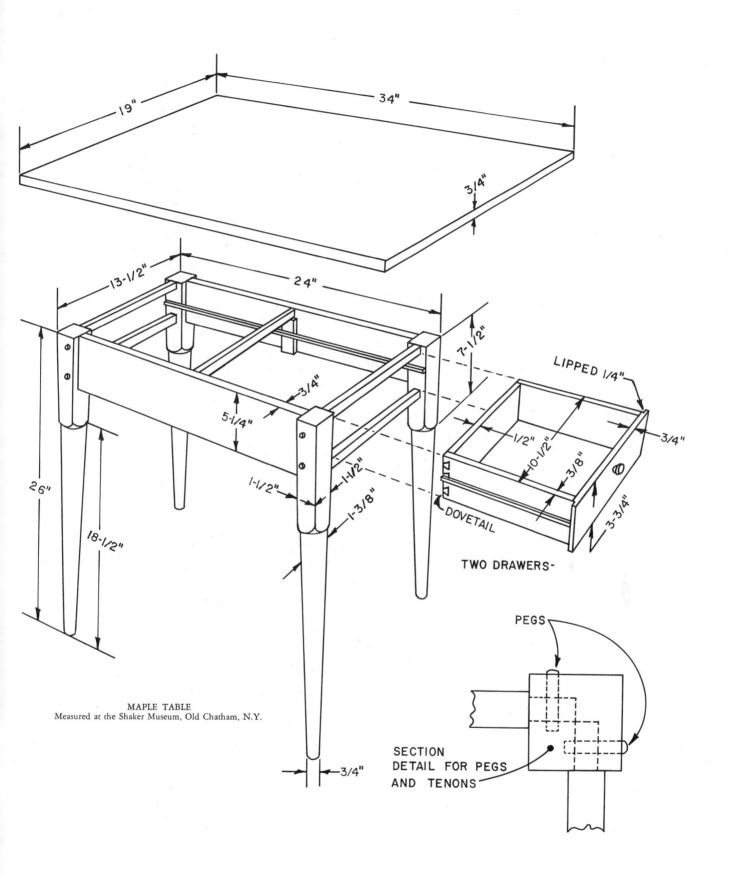

19"

34"

3/4"

13-1/2"

24"

7-1/2"

LIPPED 1/4"

3/4"

1/2"

10-1/2"

3/8"

3/4"

3/4"

5-1/4"

26"

18-1/2"

1-1/2"

1-1/2"

1-3/8"

DOVETAIL

3-3/4"

TWO DRAWERS-

3/4"

PEGS

SECTION
DETAIL FOR PEGS
AND TENONS

MAPLE TABLE
Measured at the Shaker Museum, Old Chatham, N.Y.

CHEST OF DRAWERS

Here's what happened when the Shakers discarded their lidded chest tops and started to design full chests of drawers. This handsome chest of pumpkin pine was built at Harvard, Massachusetts. It bears the inscription: "Built by Elder Joseph Myrick 1844. Finished March 8." The fine proportions and dovetailed detailing of this chest of drawers qualify it to be regarded as one of the most perfect examples of superb Shaker craftsmanship. *Photographed courtesy Fruitlands Museums, Harvard, Mass.*

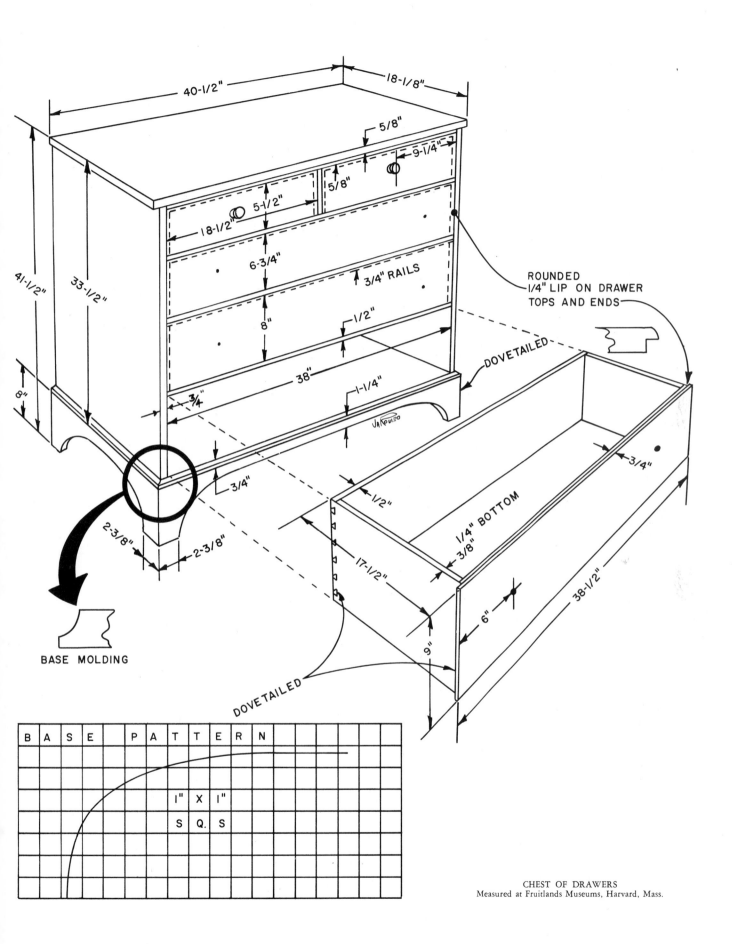

40-1/2"

18-1/8"

5/8"

9-1/4"

5/8"

5-1/2"

18-1/2"

6-3/4"

3/4" RAILS

8"

1/2"

38"

3/4"

1-1/4"

ROUNDED
1/4" LIP ON DRAWER
TOPS AND ENDS

DOVETAILED

41-1/2"

33-1/2"

8"

2-3/8"

2-3/8"

3/4"

BASE MOLDING

1/2"

1/4" BOTTOM

3/8"

3/4"

17-1/2"

6"

9"

38-1/2"

DOVETAILED

BASE PATTERN

1" X 1"

SQ. S

CHEST OF DRAWERS
Measured at Fruitlands Museums, Harvard, Mass.

193

TABLE-DESK

This table-desk was used by the Ministry of the Shirley, Massachusetts, Shakers, during the 1840's. Its delicate construction and detailing of velvet-covered writing counter suggests it may have been specially designed for one of the Eldresses. *Photographed courtesy Fruitlands Museums, Harvard, Mass.*

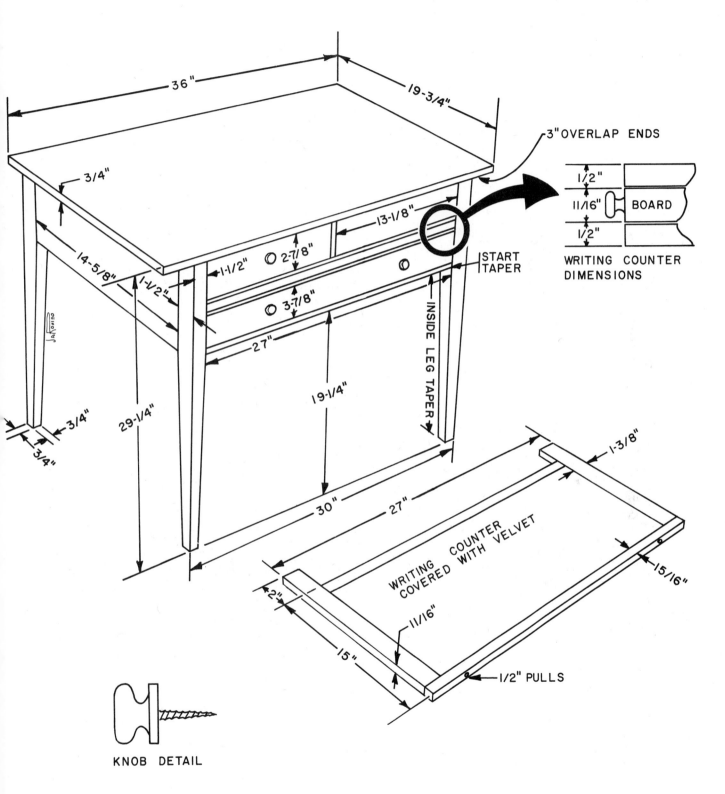

DRAWER SIDES AND BACK 1/2" THICK
FRONT 7/8"—BOTTOM 3/8"—17"DEEP

36"

19-3/4"

3/4"

3" OVERLAP ENDS

1/2"

11/16"   BOARD

1/2"

WRITING COUNTER
DIMENSIONS

13-1/8"

2-7/8"

1-1/2"

3-7/8"

START
TAPER

14-5/8"

1-1/2"

27"

INSIDE LEG TAPER

19-1/4"

3/4"

3/4"

29-1/4"

30"

27"

1-3/8"

WRITING COUNTER
COVERED WITH VELVET

15/16"

2"

11/16"

15"

1/2" PULLS

KNOB DETAIL

TABLE-DESK
Measured at Fruitlands Museums, Harvard, Mass.

195

WESTERN DRESSER

Inscribed "Daniel Sering November 9th, 1827," this walnut dresser, which was made at Union Village, Ohio, departed from the plain style which usually identified Shaker furniture of that era. The bottom embellishment of cyma scrolls and curved feet more closely resembles the work of French provincial craftsmen. Undoubtedly the design of this unusual piece was influenced by work observed outside the Shaker community. *Photographed courtesy Warren County Historical Museum, Lebanon, O.*

WESTERN DRESSER
Measured at Warren County Historical Museum, Lebanon, O.

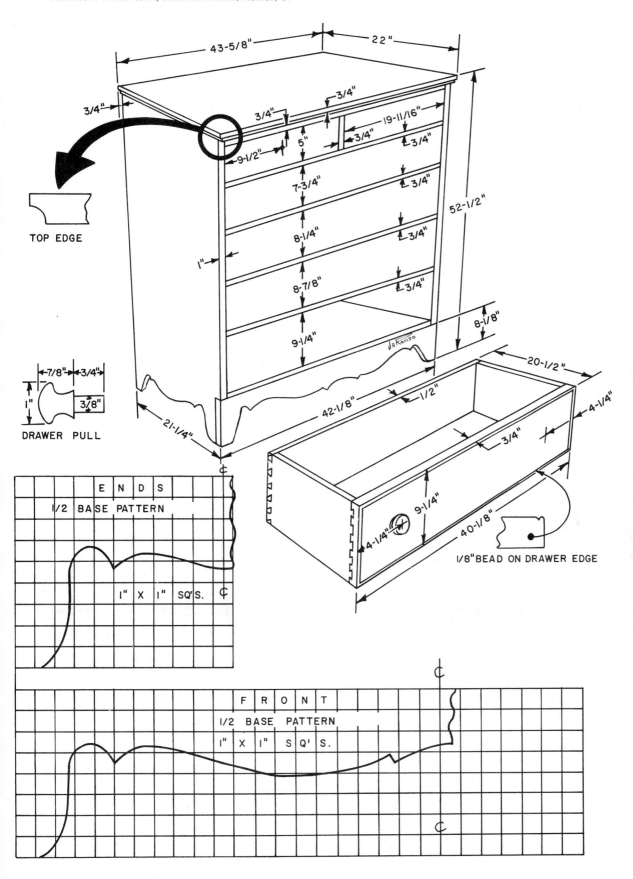

TOP EDGE

DRAWER PULL

ENDS
1/2 BASE PATTERN

1" X 1" SQ'S.

FRONT
1/2 BASE PATTERN
1" X 1" SQ'S.

1/8" BEAD ON DRAWER EDGE

197

SMALL TABLE

This delicate little side table, which was made by the Union Village, Ohio, Shakers around 1850, again demonstrates the desire of Shaker craftsmen to make their furniture as light as possible without sacrificing strength. *Photographed courtesy the Golden Lamb Inn, Lebanon, O.*

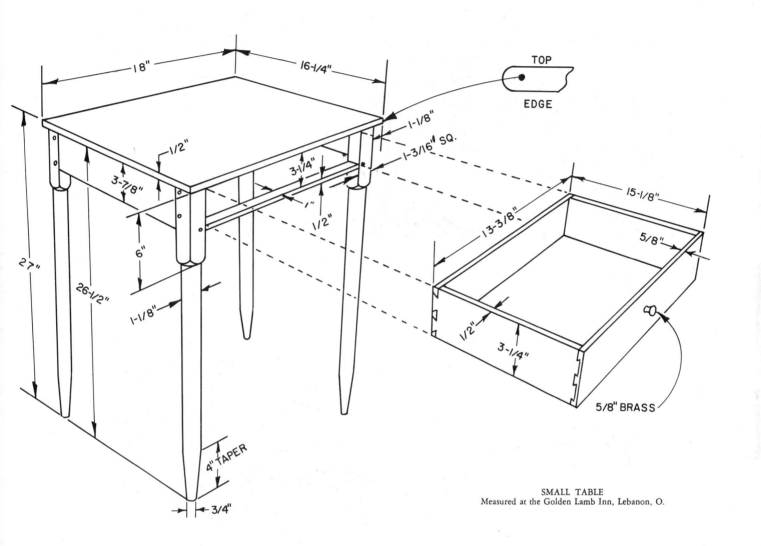

18"
16-1/4"
TOP
EDGE
1-1/8"
1/2"
1-3/16" SQ.
3-7/8"
3-1/4"
15-1/8"
13-3/8"
5/8"
27"
1"
1/2"
6"
26-1/2"
1/2"
3-1/4"
1-1/8"
4" TAPER
3/4"
5/8" BRASS

SMALL TABLE
Measured at the Golden Lamb Inn, Lebanon, O.

PORTABLE CHEST OF DRAWERS

Intricate craft detailing of the portable chest of drawers again demonstrates the patience and care of Shaker craftsmen in endeavoring to perform their work to perfection. This walnut case, with its seven dovetailed drawers, was made at Union Village, Ohio, around 1830. *Photographed courtesy Warren County Historical Museum, Lebanon, O.*

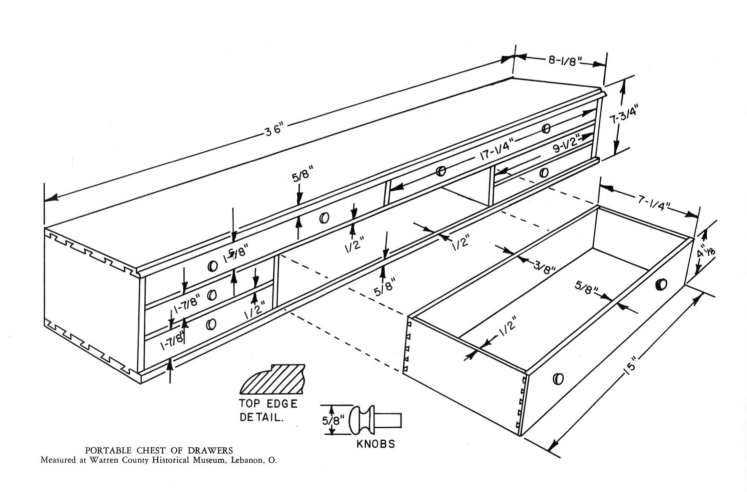

TOP EDGE DETAIL.

KNOBS

5/8"

PORTABLE CHEST OF DRAWERS
Measured at Warren County Historical Museum, Lebanon, O.

WALL CASE OF DRAWERS

This crafty case of drawers was built by the Harvard Shakers around 1840. It was probably used for sewing and knitting materials. The flawless construction, with intricate dovetailing of all drawers at the front and back, again demonstrates the skill and patience the Shakers applied to performance of all their work. *Photographed courtesy Fruitlands Museums, Harvard, Mass.*

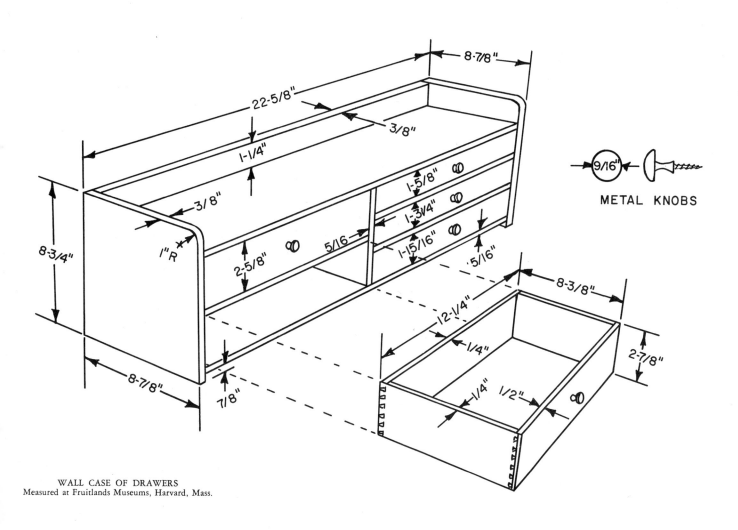

METAL KNOBS

WALL CASE OF DRAWERS
Measured at Fruitlands Museums, Harvard, Mass.

CHEST WITH CUPBOARDS

Since neatness and orderliness were prime precepts of the Shakers' way of life, the proper storage of their personal and communal possessions called for design of large chests and cupboards, which were often built to occupy entire walls from floor to ceiling. They also built movable chest-cupboards such as the one illustrated. This massive piece was made at New Lebanon, New York, around 1840. It is believed to have been used by Eldress Emma Neale. Note the ever-present steps, which were required for climbing to the top cupboards. *Photographed by Lees Studio courtesy the Shaker Museum, Old Chatham, N.Y.*

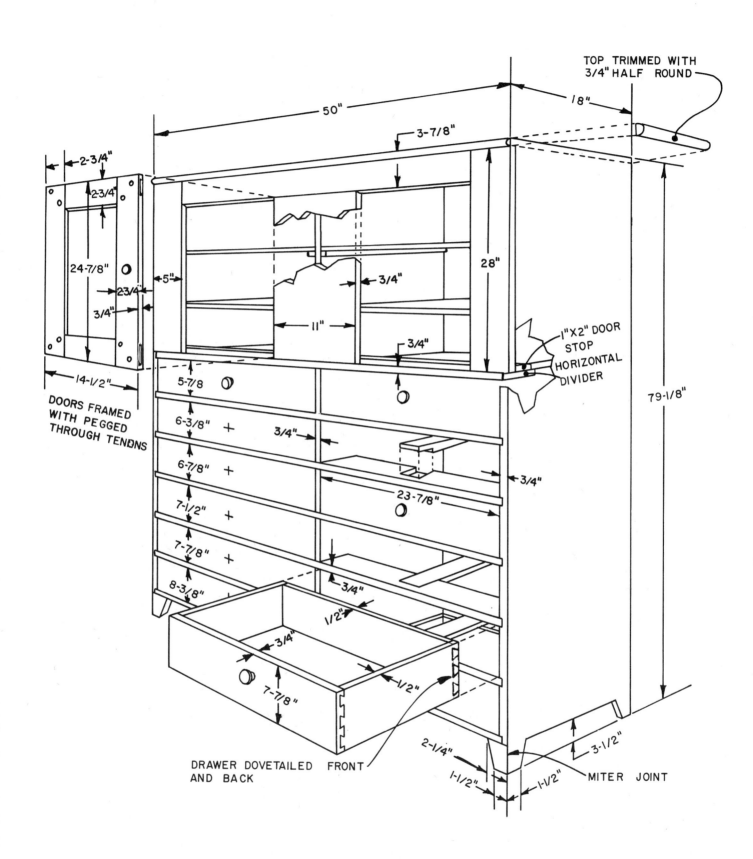

CHEST WITH CUPBOARDS
Measured at the Shaker Museum, Old Chatham, N.Y.

203

INDEX

Italicized page numbers indicate illustrations on that page. The abbreviation *(meas. draw.)* after an italicized page number indicates an explanatory measured drawing for use in analyzing or reproducing a particular piece.